Detached

A Memoir

Bridgette Pearce

W. Brand Publishing
NASHVILLE, TENNESSEE

Copyright © 2020 Bridgette Pearce.

All rights reserved. No part of this publication may be reproduced, distributed or transmitted in any form or by any means, including photocopying, recording, or other electronic or mechanical methods, without the prior written permission of the publisher, except in the case of brief quotations embodied in critical reviews and certain other noncommercial uses permitted by copyright law. For permission requests, write to the publisher, addressed "Attention: Permissions Coordinator," at the email below.

j.brand@wbrandpub.com

W. Brand Publishing

www.wbrandpub.com

Cover design by designchik.net

Photography by: Candace Brecht, Candace Brecht Photography.

Detached: a memoir/Bridgette Pearce—1st ed.

Available in Paperback, Kindle, and eBook formats.

Paperback ISBN: 978-1-950385-31-7

eBook ISBN 978-1-950385-32-4

Library of Congress Control Number: 2020935989

DISCLAIMER

I have tried to recreate events, locales, and conversations from memory. My memories and perspectives may be different than other peoples', but everything in this book is based on my experience and vision through my personal lens only. In order to maintain their anonymity in some instances, I have changed the names of individuals and places. I may have changed some identifying characteristics and details such as physical properties, occupations, and places of residence.

CONTENTS

Acknowledgements .... *vii*

Chapter 1: In My Life 1

Chapter 2: The Parallel Universe 11

Chapter 3: Of Generations, Three 25

Chapter 4: Que Sera, Sera 33

Chapter 5: The Wonder Years 43

Chapter 6: A Family, Deconstructed 59

Chapter 7: I Want a Divorce 71

Chapter 8: Go Your Own Way 95

Chapter 9: The Aftermath 109

Chapter 10: A Little Song, a Little Dance 127

Chapter 11: Yes and No 141

Chapter 12: The Endless Circle 163

About the Author 181

ACKNOWLEDGEMENTS

Detached: A Memoir was definitely not my endeavor alone, and there are many people who deserve my heartfelt thanks for accompanying me on this journey.

Tye, Kolt, and Kennedy: My beautiful children, my soul, my purpose. May you always know that sometimes the best road is the one you pave yourself. Be proud of your roots and make no apologies. Our story makes us who we are. Those who love you will never judge. Always follow the fire in your soul. . .and know that I love you to the ends of the earth and beyond.

My dearest friends (you know who you are): You have made the story of my life. Thank you for loving and supporting me through my journey. Thank you for being the family I always needed.

Shelley Moench-Kelly: Wow. Where do I even begin? You appeared in my life as an unexpected angel. You brought my story to life, you believed in me, you inspired me. The praise I have for you is endless. I am your biggest fan. With all my heart, thank you Shelley.

JuLee Brand: Thank you for believing in my story. I am so very honored to be associated with W. Brand Publishing. Your talent is unmatched.

Candace Brecht and Lexie Padgett: You both are so extremely talented, and you helped give my story a platform. Thank you for being available and willing to help me create this project.

CHAPTER 1

In My Life

I turned ten years old on June 3rd, just as the last days of spring turned warm to welcome summer.

My bedroom was on the top floor of a two-story dove gray house with a white picket fence around it. The other bedroom upstairs served as my mom's sewing and craft room, but I'd sneak into it and lie spread-eagled on the shag-carpeted floor to take naps after school before she came home from work. I couldn't do that on my twin bed. Our lawn butted up against a used brick walkway that led from the driveway to a carved mahogany front door with leaded glass inserts at eye level. Our house set far back from the little two-lane road that after a few miles ran into the city proper. Even though we were in the suburbs, our neighborhood felt as if it was smack in the center of the country, and our nearest neighbor was at least an acre away. "Close enough to be neighborly, far enough to have privacy," my granddad always said.

This life—this quiet life—was what my mom and I loved about living where we did. We were close enough to the city but out in the country far enough so that we had our own piece of the American dream.

My mom, Jeannie, was a brilliant, sought-after hairstylist in Washington, D.C., and would take the Metro rail into the city three days a week. Her clients were, for the most part, glamorous women in the world of politics, entertainment, and society; and she'd come home with stories of the rich and famous. And other times, stories of the ordinary and not-so-famous.

"Bridge, honey," she squealed as she came in the back door, dumping her purse on the counter and kicking off her shoes.

"Hi Mommy." I ran to her and gave her a hug. She smelled of Jean Nate and cigarettes.

"Bridgette, you'll never guess who I styled today! Mrs. So-and-so. And you know how when you see her on TV, she looks so tall? Baby, she's only as tall as my nose! She's TINY! And get THIS."

Mom lowered her face to meet mine. Her eyes glinted with mischief.

"She wears. . .a lady toupée!"

It was too late. Mom screeched in fits of laughter and grabbed my arm for support and she bent over as the peals continued. Her long, frosted pink polished nails impaled my arm as her laughter turned into intermittent giggles. I guess it was similar to someone sneezing and stomping a foot at the same time.

There were also horror stories of perms gone bad, color correction nightmares, and grannies with pure, white, gossamer hair who wanted to recapture the raven black, thick curly hair of their youths. This time with her was a ritual for us, even if the stories were ones I'd heard before.

Mom and I were two against the world. I didn't know my father, but as the saying goes, you can't miss what you don't know.

In the weeks leading up to my tenth birthday, I found myself thinking of markers of time.

For the first time in my life.

This is the last week I'll be one-digit old.

This is the last time I'll watch The Sound of Music *as a nine-year-old.*

I wonder how being ten years old will feel?

I'm going to be all grown up!

I'd never had these thoughts before, but they'd pop up during my day...at school, in the evening after dinner when the house was quiet, and as I awakened in the morning to the beams of sunlight piercing my bedroom curtains.

I know my mom planned a surprise party for the weekend following my big day. I saw little signs all around the house. She was just so busy with her job that she didn't have time to be as careful as full-time stay-at-home moms in hiding their kids' surprise party efforts.

I found cellophane wrappers in the kitchen trash bin that surrounded bent cardstock backing that read "30-count ivory linen embossed dining place cards."

And a crumpled to-do list in the junk drawer by the pantry that read:

30 party hats
2 Large packs of balloons

Plastic knives/forks/spoons
Gold metallic markers
Pink tulle
Ribbon
Balloon clown
Magician

My birthday was actually on a Tuesday night, and Mom cornered me a week beforehand.

"Bridgette, honey, the whole family is coming over for your birthday on Saturday! I've gotten permission to take the afternoon off, so we can have the party here. I'll make your favorite dinner. . .spaghetti and meatballs! And we'll have strawberry shortcake with pound cake and lots of glazed strawberries with fresh, homemade whipped cream!"

"Mommy, thank you! I'm so excited! I can't wait!" I threw my arms around her and she hugged me tightly. I didn't let on that I knew she had something bigger planned.

"My little princess is growing up," she said as she kissed my cheek. Her voice broke a little and she hugged me tighter.

"Mommy, I'm only 10! There's lots of time to live . . . you're like, 90 years old, right?"

She instantly released me, a look of false shock and horror on her face.

"Bridgette! That's not a very nice thing to say!"

And she got back at me with a tickle fight.

§

The day was here. It was a little cloudy outside but still bright, as if the sun would break through the clouds if the Earth shook the sleep out of its eyes.

"Honey, honey, I love you! Happy birthday! Get dressed and come on down," Mom yelled from the kitchen.

I got dressed in my favorite yellow cotton blouse with tiny bumblebees embroidered all over it, and my denim Capri pants and white sneakers.

"Well, there's my birthday girl!" my granddad exclaimed as he scooped me up in his arms and twirled me around until I got a little dizzy. He hugged me and kissed me before setting me back on my feet.

My grandmother sat quietly at the kitchen table, beaming proudly at her "birthday pancakes" with fresh Maine blueberries and maple syrup. There was a small plate with three pancakes stacked up and the number "10" laid out in blueberries on top. "Come on, young lady, eat up before they get cold!" she said, smiling and motioning me over.

"Granddad and I want to take you to the movies," she started. "That new movie about fighter pilots with Tom Cruise is supposed to be really action-packed."

"Oh my gosh! REALLY?!?" I couldn't believe it. Between Mom's work schedule and my school schedule and activities, we never had time to go to the movies together. And now I was going to go to a real theater and order popcorn. . .and maybe malt balls or Raisinets.

"Well, slowpoke, not if you don't finish your breakfast and comb your hair. Now move it!" Granddad joked.

I was up the stairs and down again in a flash and, before I knew it, was standing in line at the theater with my grandparents. The movie was larger than life and I wanted to be Tom Cruise's best friend.

All three of us ended up laughing so hard that I almost choked on a piece of popcorn. That was all I ordered. Popcorn. A small popcorn. I almost forgot for a second that a surprise party awaited me back at the house, and I wanted to save room for cake and ice cream.

"Bridgette, that was so exciting! Did you like it? What do you think about all the whirls and twirls he did in that jet? Did you know that if you're not trained as a fighter pilot and you go up in one of those things, you could throw up and pass out!" Granddad laughed.

"NO! Oh my gosh, Granddad, please no!" I cried. I worried about my hair, my clothes, and jet! All that cleanup! He winked at me. But that didn't stop me from worrying just a little.

As we drove home toward what I knew would be the party to end all parties, I wondered how big my cake would be, and if each layer would be a different flavor? What flavor ice cream would we have? Did Mom manage to get a balloon artist *and* a magician?

Granddad turned the corner onto our street and when I looked up, my heart dropped into my stomach.

DETACHED

The only car in the driveway was my mom's. The mailbox was bare. . .I'd hoped for some balloons or a little unicorn flag or something. Anything that signaled a party lay ahead. As we entered the house, I smelled food cooking and heard Mom working in the kitchen. Muted conversation partnered with kitchen cleanup echoed through the hallway.

"Is that the birthday girl?" I heard my Aunt Fran ask in a sing-songy way as she turned the corner to trap me in a bear hug. Her perfume was really strong. I felt as if I would pass out because she wouldn't let go.

"Hi Aunt Fran, thank you for coming." I smiled weakly as I entered the kitchen still in her clutches. My uncles, Joe and Pat, sat at the table. They were in their early 20s, and the looks on their faces spoke volumes.

I would rather be in detention.

"I'll be right back," I said quietly, and ran up the stairs to my room. I flung myself on the bed and cursed myself for dreaming too much. It wasn't like me, and now I knew why.

Silly. Silly. Stupid. Geez.

I buried my face in the cool percale sheets and realized I had a lot to be thankful for. I was always mature for my age, as most only children were, so this little disappointment wasn't as devastating as it might have been for others. But still. It stung a little.

Pop.

Ugh. It must be the neighbor's old car backfiring again.

I opened my window and looked out into the backyard.

"SURPRISE!"

I was so startled that I stepped backward and almost fell.

On our lawn stood what looked to be fifty of my classmates, teachers, and family, all wearing sparkly party hats, twirling noisemakers and lighting festive sparklers . . . while they screamed up to me,

"HAPPY BIRTHDAY!"

I'd never run down a flight of stairs so quickly in my life.

§

When you hear women say an event—such as a wedding proposal, the birth of a child, or a professional acknowledgement—made them feel as special as a princess, you can add to that list my tenth birthday party.

In the now cloudless Saturday afternoon sky, I emerged from our kitchen sliding doors onto the terraced patio and was immediately engulfed with a group hug by the people closest to me in my young life.

Uncle Joe and Uncle Pat were laughing at me.

"Oh man, you should have seen your FACE!" Pat cried.

I looked out onto the sea of familiar faces as the crowd began serenading me.

I saw a slender arm waving at me from the patio corner. It was Mom, directing me to the cake.

As I made my way through the crowd and got closer to Mom, friends parted to clear the path. At the end of it, I was greeted with a three-tiered strawberry cake with mountains of whipped cream and gold nonpareils dotting the surface. The cake topper was a blonde princess figurine that looked just like Sleeping Beauty.

"Bridgette, honey, don't forget to make a wish!" I heard my granddad say from a few feet behind me.

Mom lit the candles as all the guests finished singing, and I inched closer to her. I'll never forget how she looked that day...she was so happy...but there was something else.

A sadness in her eyes that I couldn't understand.

Still, she smiled broadly and gathered me close to her side.

"Everyone, everyone, let's let Bridgette have her wish, OK? Sweetheart, just take your time. Make your wish, and blow out the candles. You only turn ten once!"

I looked at her and she side-hugged me and kissed my head.

The crowd became silent.

And suddenly, my ears started ringing.

I must have eaten too much popcorn, I thought. *I hope I don't get sick.*

And as I took a deep breath to blow out those ten candles, everything turned gray and I felt my legs buckle as I floated into silent darkness.

CHAPTER 2

The Parallel Universe

I woke up sore and headachy, spread-eagled on the shag-carpeted floor. My right arm was outstretched and clutching. . . nothing. . .and my mouth was open in silent speech to someone I couldn't see.

The sun shone blindingly into the room and made angular streaks on the shag carpeting and my legs, and I was momentarily unsure of my surroundings, still in a half-awake daze from the fairy-tale dream that lingered in my mind. There was no bed with percale sheets, no white picket fence. No aunts or uncles. No grandparents and no movies. No cake. No party at all.

Oh, that's right.

This is what's real.

My tenth birthday party with my family and friends in a beautiful house with balloons tied to the patio rafters and a three-tiered birthday cake. . .was just a dream.

In my reality, in this awake reality, I had my own room as I did in my dream. But that's where most of the similarities ended. I slept on a mattress on the floor and kept a flashlight for doing my homework or reading when it got dark and our electricity was out. This apartment (one of the several we lived in) came fitted with a few pieces of furniture, so I had a little dresser and a chair. I made a desk with some cinder blocks and a piece of wood, and I covered the bottom half of the bare window with black construction paper so if anyone tried to peer in, they might see the top of my head. My closet was about six feet wide and had a proper wooden door on it, not folding doors or flimsy double plywood doors. When you opened the door, there was three feet of immediate space right in front of you, then three feet to the left for stuff you rarely reached for.

Sometimes I'd hide in the left side of the closet when the screaming got bad.

I heard sounds from outside my bedroom door, the almost-normal sounds of my mom making her way through the kitchen. I heard a cabinet slam shut and mugs clinking in the sink. I say almost normal because the sounds were normal; the vision was not. Anyone looking at our kitchen would instantly notice the faded linoleum cupboard doors on loose hinges, and mugs with dried coffee rings in them and murky, thick coffee remains in their bottoms. Ceramic dishes that once littered the sink and counters made way for knock-off Chinet plates because our water and electricity weren't always guaranteed. Silverware was also a thing of the past, instead replaced with plastic forks and knives from whatever fast-food restaurant my friends could grab a few extra sets from after they finished their meals on nights when their moms didn't have time or energy to cook. I could never bring myself to walk into a restaurant and grab silverware if I wasn't actually having a meal, and God knows we could never afford it. I was always careful to use them only when I absolutely needed to, using a few drops of water to clean them off and using them as long as I could before they'd shatter.

Our kitchen table was a folding card table with three mismatched folding chairs shoved to one side to make room for us to squeeze our way to the mini fridge that was perched on a plastic milk crate. The only food we ever had in the fridge was fruit, sometimes milk, and leftover canned ravioli or SpaghettiOs with a paper towel secured by a rubber band over the can top. The kitchen walls were covered with wallpaper that depicted hummingbirds flitting around vibrant hibiscus flowers that, if you weren't quite awake—or lucid—took on a macabre, blood-spattered appearance. The floor was multicolored shades of avocado green rectangles that fit together like Tetris blocks, and the single window was painted shut and sported a lace café curtain and valance that gave some privacy from the road but not much shade.

"Bridgette, come on, you're going to be late for school," Mom said as she grabbed the Folgers instant coffee jar from the countertop. She filled the mug with tap water, shook the dark crystals into it, and stirred it with her finger.

"Mommy, did you sleep OK?" I asked, hoping she might be trying to cover up my birthday surprise by acting as if today was just any old day.

"No, sweetheart. I have a killer headache. Do we have any Tylenol?"

My hopes sank a little, but the day was young. My own headache was gone now, but I knew Mom's headaches weren't really headaches at all, but rather hangovers. And they weren't kind. I ran to the bathroom and found the expired bottle of Tylenol and brought two back to the kitchen. Mom downed them dry and went back to bed just as I left for school.

And that was all that happened at home in my awake reality on the morning of my tenth birthday.

§

"HAPPY BIRTHDAY, BRIDGETTE!" my classmates yelled as I entered my homeroom. There was a gigantic cupcake on my desk and my teacher, Miss Shapiro, lit the single, glittery silver candle with her royal blue Bic lighter. On her desk sat two matching rectangular Tupperware sheet "cake takers" with harvest gold bases and frosted opaque covers. I touched the cover as I strolled past her desk pretending to smell the cupcakes. It felt solid. Permanent.

Only rich people buy Tupperware, I thought. *The rest of us just wrap everything in tinfoil and hope for the best.*

Inside were regular-size cupcakes for the rest of the class. These were vanilla cake with white frosting and chocolate jimmies. It was customary in our class to celebrate this way; the birthday girl or boy got the large cupcake and everyone else got a regular one. It was easier than trying to cut a sheet cake and dole it out to dozens of kids. . .and to await the mess that came after.

My favorite flavor was yellow cake with buttercream icing and rainbow sprinkles. Miss Shapiro was a forty-something, single lady who had a tabby cat named Ginger, a knack for baking, and big, blonde, out-to-there hair that never moved. At the beginning of the school year, she asked the class to fill out a little survey with questions such as "what is your favorite animal?"

"what is your favorite book?" and "what is your favorite cake/frosting combo?" I smiled at the memory.

"Make a wish, Bridgette, and don't tell anyone what it is!" Miss Shapiro leaned over to the cupcake, then instinctively backed off. A single spark from a flame would be the end of her hair.

I wish Mommy would get better, I thought, squeezing my eyes shut and blowing one big puff of air toward the candle. I opened my eyes when I smelled the acrid smoke from the extinguished flame assaulting my nose. My eyes started to water and everyone laughed as they clapped for me.

"What'd ya wish for! Tell us! Tell us!" my classmates screamed. I looked at their faces, so filled with innocence and curiosity. A few were jumping up and down, unable to contain their excitement.

"I wished that my granddad would take me to see *Top Gun* this weekend!" I laughed.

"Oh, you LUCKY DUCK! I wanna see that SO bad! I wanna be a pilot when I grow up!" one boy said excitedly.

"Ohhh! Tom Cruise is dreamy!" another girl cried.

I'd staved off the pack. Satisfied that I'd clearly be the first one in the class to go to the movie, each classmate took a cupcake from the Tupperware container and walked back to their desks. *Another bullet dodged,* I thought. The rest of the day was uneventful and I couldn't concentrate on my studies. Most of me knew better, but part of me wondered if I *would* come home to a party like the one I dreamed of.

§

In this awake reality, the day was sunny but harbored a little breeze that chilled me as I waited for my granddad to pick me up.

"Mommy, I'm home!" I yelled as I unlocked the apartment door. The space was quiet and the apartment was illuminated only by daylight that streamed through the windows. Even though it was only 3:30 p.m., the apartment felt dark and. . . dead. I wondered if the electricity had been shut off again or if there was still a chance that I might have a party, even if it was just Mom and me. *Maybe. . . maybe it feels dead because fifteen people are hiding in my room waiting for me to open the door?*

I walked down the hallway to the kitchen and found a birthday card with Snoopy and Woodstock on its front propped open on the little card table without its envelope. Woodstock was flying around Snoopy as he slept atop his red doghouse. It was a birthday card, but it really wasn't. Next to it was a Snickers bar that was a little smushed, probably from being in the bottom of Mom's purse.

I opened the card slowly, thinking. . .hoping. . .that maybe Mom had taped a $5 bill to the inside.

Nope.

It read: *"Happy birthday, Bridgette. I love you, Mom."* I took it and the candy bar into my empty room and hid them in my dresser.

"Mom?" I called out.

There was no answer.

I turned the corner to the living room to find her passed out cold on the couch.

§

My mom was somewhere in the middle of seven children, and the family always described her as the fun one, the life of every party...a brilliant, unpredictable sprite. She was beautiful and glamorous and loved to pretend that she was a famous singer to an audience that consisted of her six siblings, my grandmother, and my beloved granddad.

"Oh Bridgette," my aunt Fran started, "your mom was always the most outgoing, funny person in the family. I think she got it from Daddy." Her green eyes twinkled as she scrunched up her cheeks to reveal a million-watt smile. Mom had gone grocery shopping and Aunt Fran showed up unexpectedly a few days after my birthday. Surprising Mom was the best way of catching her, because any attempts at scheduling visits or family dinners proved too much of a commitment, too much of a stressor. Plus, try as she might to ready herself for a family event, her insecurities always got the best of her and she'd retreat to the safety of her room to drown her feelings in whatever substance she had handy. When she was sober enough, she worked as a hairstylist in Washington, D.C. That was another small detail of my birthday dream that was true, as was the fact that my granddad was, in the dream, as beautiful and full of love as he was in real life.

Aunt Fran and I sat in the kitchen that Saturday, sharing a tuna sandwich and a glass of milk. She twirled a silver ring around her finger as she shared family stories with me; and from time to time, took my hand in hers and squeezed it, as if to say "you're loved, and I hope you know that."

"Aunt Fran, what was Mommy like when she was my age?"

She snorted as an immediate memory came flooding back. "Bridgette, I will tell you one story about Jeannie that will tell you who she is at heart . . ." Aunt Fran's voice trailed off, and in one moment her mood changed from lighthearted to brokenhearted. "Bridgette, you know she loves you more than anything, right? And she worries about your safety. . . because. . ."

She stopped suddenly and took a huge bite of her sandwich. She quickly chased it down with a giant gulp of milk, as if to mask any outward show of emotion. The distraction cleared her thoughts.

"Where was I? Oh yes. . .when I was about your age, your grandmother was supposed to be the school chaperone for one of my classes. As it turned out, Gran'ma couldn't make it, so Jeannie stepped up. The teacher's instructions on the chalkboard were for the students to make as many words as they could out of the words *Merry Christmas*."

I started thinking silently:
Shy
Christ
Mist
His
Rim
Cherry
Him
Mast
Stem . . .

"And the class was pretty slow," Aunt Fran continued, "so your mom wrote the first word she could think of on the chalkboard in huge letters: *SHIT*."

We both broke into squeals of laughter, and milk went up my nose.

"When Jeannie was still in high school, she could command the attention of the entire school just by walking into a room. It was so magical. She just had this. . .this confidence, you know? She lit up the room." Aunt Fran smiled wistfully and squeezed my hand again before looking away, out the painted-shut window and beyond. At nothing. Maybe just the sky.

At that moment, Mom came home loaded with three paper bags of groceries and plopped them on the counter. As she turned to face me, Fran stood up and gently hugged her.

The look on Mom's face was one of surprise—maybe even fear—and she stood stiffly in Fran's embrace before finally letting go and returning a long bear hug to her little sister.

"Oh Frannie," Mom said as she took my aunt's face in her hands. She looked deeply into her sister's eyes and started to weep quietly.

"It's OK, Jeannie. It's OK. I love you."

I crept out of the kitchen as quietly as I could and retreated to my room. Aunt Fran didn't leave until after midnight.

§

My mother found out she was pregnant *with* me. . .became an unwed mother *of* me when she was just seventeen years old. As far as anyone could remember, that's when her problems began. There was no way she would *not* have me, and no way she would ever give me up. So, the only way to cope with her new life was to try and escape it. My grandmother was a surly type, always had been, and she was the polar opposite of my granddad. Aunt Fran told me that Granddad loved my mother "the most, even though he loved all his children with all his heart and would die protecting them." Every year at Christmas, even in the worst of times, Mom would make a plate of homemade chocolate chip cookies for Granddad. It was all she had. It was all she could do. And his eyes lit up every time he'd see his favorite daughter. The cookies mattered a lot to Granddad because he knew what an effort it took Mom to make them. They would sit together in the dining room and share cookies and milk and talk about silly things that made my Mom giggle like I'd never seen.

And this yearly ritual only served to infuriate my grandmother; it brought out the ugliest side of her already cynical self. She didn't even like my mother. She disliked my mom for as long as anyone could remember, and was in the nasty habit of constantly talking down to Mom and belittling her. No one knew why. Gran'ma was only ever happy when she settled down in her recliner to watch TV with a box of Ho Hos and a big glass of iced tea.

Mom's deep insecurity surely stemmed from the loveless relationship with her own mother, and I know it's why she chose the coping mechanisms she did to try and drown out the pain.

I always knew that she loved me as deeply as Granddad loved her, but she rarely showed it because she was so sick and her emotions were all over the map. When she did show affection, she showered me with hugs and kisses and promises that all my dreams would come true.

As long as she was lucid.

I never lived in a proper, permanent house that was all mine until I got married. Mom and I always lived in apartments and we moved frequently. Even though in grade school and middle school I would spend many nights at my grandparents' house, it was like sleeping at a friend's house: you loved the new environment, but you knew that you'd eventually have to return to your own home. There was rarely a feeling of permanence, and Mom would move frequently because of back rent due or trouble that her boyfriends would cause.

None of these men were sad or quiet drunks and substance abusers. Mom had long-term boyfriends, but they would end up in the same way: abusive, loud, obnoxious, and violent. She craved acceptance, love, and kindness, and these men came through at the very beginnings of their relationships. Each one was her savior, her knight in shining armor. Aside from one man that we lived with for a brief time, we never lived with them; they all came to live in our apartment, in our *home*.

And when the inevitable beatings came with each man-child that invaded our space, my mother would plead for forgiveness and mercy, time and again returning to the hands that beat her into unconsciousness and rendering even more unconscionable terrors when she couldn't fight back.

§

"Bridgette, Bridgette, honey, open the door!" my mother hissed frantically. I always locked my door because guests had a way of entering without knocking.

"Mommy, what is it?" I asked as I let her in.

She'd been crying and put her finger to her lips before leaning against the door and clicking the lock closed. She pulled my dresser in front of the door to block it before turning to face me.

Her breathing was raspy and shallow and I noticed a trickle of blood tracing a thin path down her cheek.

"Mommy! What happened?"

"Shh, shh, honey, just be quiet for Mommy, OK? Let's just be quiet." She grabbed my hand and dragged me into the closet and shut the door. We scooted to the left side of the closet and pushed all the clothes in front of the door. She motioned to me to put on my boots and whispered that if anyone came through the door, I was to start kicking with all my might, and that she would, too. And that we wouldn't stop kicking until our attacker was on the ground.

"Bridgette, we have to protect ourselves, OK? Promise me you'll do as I say! When we get him down, make sure he's on his stomach and I'll sit on his back. Then you call the police, OK? Who's my girl? I love you, baby. That's a good girl. That's my sweet girl."

She embraced me tightly and rocked back and forth, me in my pajamas and boots and she in shorts, a T-shirt, and sneakers. And Jean Nate. Another dream carryover. No matter what shape she was in, Mom always wore Jean Nate.

Her eyes were clear and fierce; I couldn't see or smell the telltale signs of drink or drugs, so I knew she was sober.

"Mommy, why did he hurt you? Why is he so mean to you?!?" I pleaded.

"Sweetie, he is just stressed out. And yes, he hurt me. Sometimes you have to fight back, though. Let's just be as quiet as church mice, OK? Then maybe he'll leave."

Hours passed. I don't know how many, but I was so exhausted from being on high alert and ready to strike at any moment that I fell asleep. I woke up alone.

The closet door and my bedroom door were wide open and the apartment still. My heart felt as if it would beat right out of my body because I didn't know what happened to Mom.

I made my way into the hallway. The front door was shut and the kitchen and living room were empty, as was our single bathroom. There was one room left behind a closed door.

Her bedroom.

And as I turned the doorknob and peeked into the pre-dawn gloom, I saw my mother in the arms of the man. They bore the angelic, peaceful faces of babies in slumber.

An empty bottle of Jack Daniel's lay between them.

BRIDGETTE PEARCE

CHAPTER 3

Of Generations, Three

My aunt Fran was the youngest of my mom's sisters, and because I was an only child, she was like an older sister to me. A nonjudgmental, love-you-to-the-moon-and-back sister without the drama that real sisters usually share because of jealousy, insecurity, and familial pecking order.

When she visited, we would get so involved in playing records and dancing that hours would pass in what seemed like a few seconds. Sometimes, we'd go to the park and people watch.

"Bridge, look at that guy." Fran grabbed my hand and scrunched in close to my face, pointing at a guy walking his dog. Her hand was between our chins and I could barely see her pointing at him.

"I'll bet he spoils his dog and his wife's jealous!" she said with a snort and a giggle.

"Do you think he has kids?" I asked.

"Nah. If he did, they'd be with him walking the dog, I think. Or maybe, maybe you're right! Maybe this is his quiet time!"

I looked back at the man. He was slender and wore sneakers, Levi's, a flannel shirt, and a baseball cap. He sported some superthick Coke-bottle glasses and stood patiently while his little dog, a beagle, stopped to sniff some dandelions in the grass.

"Come on, buddy, let's go," Levi man said as he clicked his tongue at the dog, who pulled on his leash as if to say, "Aww dad, just five more minutes, please?"

We sat together on the bench, my aunt Fran and me, holding hands and making up stories for everyone that passed us by.

"Sweetie, I have something for you. But you can't tell your mom, OK? It'll be our little secret!"

She started rummaging in her purse and hid something in her hand.

"OK, close your eyes and hold out your hand! Don't peek!" she squealed.

I held out my hand and closed my eyes tightly. The sun was so bright that all I saw was neon orange.

There. It was done.

I opened my eyes and looked in my hand. It was a brand-new package of Goody hair barrettes with little multicolored rhinestones that looked like diamonds.

"Now Bridge, you know you should never lie. But this is important. If your mom asks you where you got these, please don't tell her I gave them to you, OK? Maybe tell her that all the cheerleaders have them, which is true, and leave it at that."

I understood immediately. When I was very young, around the age of four, mom wasn't affected as much by her addictions as she was when I was an older child of eight to thirteen years old. There were more times that she was sober enough to show love when I was younger, but they became rarer as the addiction took greater hold of her. She became more narcissistic as a result of years of demons catching up with her and, as a result, I had to remember the tender times in memories instead of current actions.

The act of giving was such an intimate one, and my relationship with my mother was unpredictable. On a good day, on a lucid, sober day, Mom would love to see me bonding with her younger sister, not as a replacement for her, but as a relationship that she knew was healthy for me. On a bad day, she could take relationship in all its innocence as an attack on her abilities as a parent, or worse, as an attempt to play favorites. Neither of these was accurate, but we had to take precautions.

The same was true with my grandparents, but in a different way. Mom knew how they each felt about me, and had no problem with it. Between them, however, I had to walk on eggshells.

My granddad was a high-ranking naval officer and the kindest, most selfless person I've ever known in my entire life. He was not only a talented engineer but a brilliant attorney as well, and had a work ethic that topped any C-level executive I've ever met. He was as handsome as a young Henry Fonda and had a heart as true and pure as Fred Rogers. But despite the fact that he made a good living, you'd never guess it from the conditions my grandparents lived in. They owned a little brick house that was built in the 1930s that greeted you with three shallow concrete steps bordered by iron handrails on either side. There were two street-facing dormer windows and an attic, which is where I lived when I stayed there. It was well tended on the outside, but a messy, stale disaster on the inside.

And it was all due to my grandmother. For as long as I can remember, she was like a wicked stepmother, only older. When I was very young, she was actually nice to me. Her worst trait in life was her overwhelming laziness. She was lonely, too, and her life was stagnant. And when I got older, she started getting mean toward me. It wasn't just directed at my mother and Granddad anymore.

And before I could say anything, she'd stormed out of the room to plant her body on the ancient Barcalounger in the living room and switch on the TV to *One Life to Live*. What lay before me was at least a two-hour task: mountains of mismatched pottery mugs and ceramic plates lay strewn all over the counters and filled the sink past its brim. Nothing had been soaked, so food remained fossilized on the plates, and the old sink didn't have a disposal, so they had to be soaked in a plastic basin so the sink wouldn't get clogged. I wanted the kitchen (and the house, for that matter) to be clean and safe. It was no small task, and I knew that if I didn't tackle it, the entire living space would remain filthy and unsanitary. And there was also a part of me that realized that even when I cleaned everything to spotlessness, it wouldn't stay that way for long.

No matter what, I had to finish these chores before I was allowed to see my granddad, who was the light of my life. And I would do anything for him, endure any hardship. He stayed out of sight, out of her way, from the minute he came home every night to the minute he left for work every morning. His life was relegated to his bedroom, but he never once complained, and no one would ever guess Granddad was anything but the loving, sincere, gentle, decent man that he was.

But my grandmother was the polar opposite of him. Her jealousy, anger, and frustration carried from my mother to my grandfather. She was horrible to him. She would order him around mercilessly and send him to the market at 10:00 p.m. at night if she ran out of Ho Hos. He always went. He never complained or retorted. But she'd still abuse him, verbally and sometimes physically...one time she even threw a metal chair down the basement steps at him.

And always at the back of her mind was me.

It was as if she could never forgive my mom for being an unwed, teenage mother, but also because Mom was blessed with timeless beauty and an incredible figure.

And she couldn't forgive me for being the product of that liaison.

"You know, Bridgette, you're a beautiful girl, just like your mother," she said one day as I was vacuuming the living room. I was caught off guard for a moment, because it was the nicest thing I'd ever heard her say. In those early years, she was never outwardly mean to me, and she actually loved me and worked to protect me, I think, when I was little. She never gave me rules; as if she expected me to know the difference between right and wrong and that I'd know what I was doing and would make the right decisions.

And then the moment was over.

"It's too bad she ruined her life, and now we're stuck with her sad life," she sneered, before consuming an entire Ho Ho in one bite. She washed it down with a gulp of Lipton ice tea from a giant mason jar. Exactly five opaque ice cube blocks filled the vessel. I'd watched her count them out as she dropped them into the narrow mouth of the jar that only she drank from. There was always a box of Ho Hos in the refrigerator but nothing much in the way of fresh food. My granddad mostly ate peanut butter and jelly sandwiches and, when my grandmother cooked, meals were always along the line of warm pork 'n' beans and boiled hot dogs or Kraft macaroni and cheese with microwaved Vienna sausages. On holidays, she'd roast a chicken and serve it up with canned gravy and boxed stuffing.

One day as I was washing dishes, praying for time to pass so I could spend the afternoon with Granddad, Gran'ma entered the kitchen to refill her iced tea jar. She startled me when she started to speak. I expected criticism of some sort, and braced myself for a tongue-lashing.

"You know, Bridgette, you don't ever have to see Junior if you don't want to. Any honorable man would've properly married your mom. She was so beautiful and could have had her pick of any young man she wanted. But she thought she was in love. He was well beneath Jeannie in every way. He was just a mechanic, had no schooling or future. All he ate was junk food and he didn't look after himself. Not like your mom. She had potential."

She snorted, which signaled the moment was over. I rarely heard any sentiments that even bordered on protective or kind. I knew this was as good as it would get, and even imagined that maybe she would pat me on the shoulder or give me a hug, but to even imagine it was an impossibility. I looked right back at her, emotionless and eye to eye.

"OK," I said quietly.

Gran'ma smoothed her housecoat and sucked in her gut, which spilled over her thighs and jiggled a lot when she walked. She smiled right at me, but it was a dead smile. It showed up from her nose down, and her eyes didn't change. It wasn't until years later that I learned what a genuine smile was. A smile that came from the heart, a smile that was true lit up your whole face, and your eyes would twinkle and the little wrinkles that grown-ups called crow's-feet would appear. Anything else was false. Staged. Fake. All the things I never wanted to be. Because even at that tender age, I knew I was nothing like my grandmother. She had no direction, no motivation, and I couldn't relate to her. I felt sad for her.

As the years wore on and I approached ten, I began to understand why my mother was the way she was. She had to learn to love, because she never knew it from her own mother; and any love she received from her beloved father was squashed into nothingness by the omniscience of the elder woman. And so her attempts to love me . . . which I know, deep down, she did . . . got buried by the lifelong insecurity she felt from her own upbringing, her own teenage pregnancy, and the failed relationships with men she trusted too much and for too long.

She didn't want fame.

She didn't want riches, fancy houses, or jewelry.

All she wanted was love.

BRIDGETTE PEARCE

CHAPTER 4

Que Sera, Sera

My earliest memories as a child were of my pet ferret. I didn't receive him as a birthday present, but as part of a July 4th celebration a month after my fourth birthday. For as rare as presents were in my life, receiving them was truly special, so I wasn't going to nitpick.

On that July morning, I knew something was up when I ran into our kitchen for breakfast. We still had ceramic plates that early on. And real glasses and metal flatware. It would be three years before the paper plates and plastic utensils even appeared.

Mom sat in the chair facing the entrance to the kitchen, a cigarette dangling from her slender fingers. In these early days of summer, she frequently wore jean shorts and form-fitting T-shirts with little cap sleeves that showed off her toned, slender arms. In those early years, she always sported a fresh mani/pedi, a fringe benefit of her work as a stylist. Back in those days, they were called beauticians. She formed an opaque outline against the early morning sun that illuminated the kitchen from behind her chair. A dark, mysterious silhouette. I couldn't see her expression.

"Well, there's my sweet girl," she said, as smoke curled in front of her eyes before it rose above her head. . .curly snakes of smoke haloed her tousled hair as she smiled and motioned for me to come closer.

It was a real smile.

As I walked closer, I peered at the table. At its center was a plate of two Hostess cupcakes. Hostess was a staple in our home, and krimpets were my absolute favorite. Also on the table was a glass of milk, and Mom had a coffee mug in front of her. As I leaned in for a hug, I smelled. . . not coffee. Something else that burned my nostrils. Acrid. I smelled it on her breath, too.

"Come here baby, give mama a kiss. Do you know what today is? It's July 4th! It's our country's birthday! I thought we'd have a little Happy Birthday USA and then tonight we can watch the fireworks!"

And then we had cupcakes for breakfast. I couldn't believe my luck. Mom peeled the frosting off the cupcake in one piece and carefully set it on the plate, then ate the cake part in four dainty bites. Then she folded the frosting circlet in half and in half again and wolfed down the sweet in one giant bite. I couldn't eat my cupcake in as few bites as she did, but I followed her lead and took sips of cold milk from my glass in between chocolatey, cakey bites and ultra-rich candy frosting bites. I was in heaven. To this day, I can't look at Hostess cupcakes without remembering that sweet summer morning.

When we finished, Mom reached behind her chair and put a big shoebox in front of me. It was the color of a brown paper bag and had a big red, white, and blue glittery stars-and-stripes bow right in the middle of the box top, which had a few holes punched into it.

I jumped when it moved.

"Go on, Bridgette, don't be scared. It's just a little thing I thought you'd like."

I sat on the floor and steadied the box between my knees and carefully removed the top. Inside was a wriggly, furry, slender creature with soft brown eyes. I'd wanted a pet for as long as I could remember, especially when I'd see the neighbor kids playing fetch with their dogs or finding cats hiding in the trees. I vaguely remember having a rabbit when I was very little, as well as a hamster and a duck, but it always seemed as if they were only around for a few days and then they were gone. I never knew exactly how they got there or how they disappeared. But I never had my very own pet.

"Mommy, what is it? Is it mine?"

"Sweetheart, it's a ferret. They're very intelligent and loving. And it's all yours. Now go play." She waved me off with the cigarette-holding hand and ashes fell into the box.

I named him Shorty. And at the end of the day when Mom came home from work, I put Shorty in my bedroom and we drove to the park to see the fireworks. Just as Mom promised.

"Mommy, is Granddad coming with us?" Even at four years old, I didn't hold my grandmother in high regard, although she hadn't yet displayed any hostility toward me. I always just felt a bad sensation when I was around her, and she was not the loving type that you expect most grandmothers to be. When she picked me up, it wasn't with a loving, gentle touch; it was mechanical. Robotic. Cold.

"No, sweetie. We're going by ourselves, and then afterward, we'll have Chinese food and then we'll go to a fun party!"

It was the first time I ever saw fireworks, and the night was unforgettable. I saw giant red chrysanthemum fireworks followed by clear sparkle whirligigs and miniature purple and blue popcorn fireworks that exploded in groupings of ten, each delayed by a second of time, like real popcorn popping on a stove. Seeing all the different rainbow colors and shapes and sizes of glittering lights in the night sky made me feel like a princess, and when I looked at Mom, I saw her smile that real smile again. I snuggled in close and she side-hugged me.

And as quickly as the dazzling show began, it ended with a raucous explosion of multiple fireworks that were so loud I had to cover my ears. Mom put her hands over mine and I could feel her body shake as she giggled.

"Come on honey, let's get dinner before we go to the party," Mom squealed as she grabbed my hand and led me back to the car.

We stopped at the local Chinese restaurant and Mom got us a booth right by the giant fluorescent fish tank. I climbed into the booth and into a booster seat... I felt very grown up. Mom ordered chicken chow mein and egg rolls. I got my very own plate and she spooned out my portion and gave me a tiny plastic packet of soy sauce with the corner cut off. I didn't remember eating in a restaurant before, so the experience was very exciting. The food smelled so yummy and at the end, we got fortune cookies and almond cookies for dessert. And a little orange wedge.

"Honey, give me your cookie. I'll read your fortune!" Mom said with a wink.

She broke the cookie in two and gave it back to me.

As I nibbled on it, she read the microscopic writing on the glossy paper strip.

"You will have great success," she said, grinning.

I got very excited. Maybe great success meant we could eat dinner here every night.

"Mommy, what does your cookie say?"

"Hmm, let's see. It says 'Beware of fool's gold.'"

"What does that mean?" I asked.

"Oh sweetie, I think something's gotten lost in translation. These fortunes are silly anyway."

She laughed and waved her hand at me. "Come on, it's party time!"

§

As a four-year-old, I didn't know what time it was when we left the restaurant, but I knew it was late. Looking back, most fireworks shows start around 9:00 at night, so I guess we must have set off for the party by 10:30. After the excitement of the fireworks wore off, my body knew it was well past my normal bedtime and I fell asleep in the car.

I was jolted awake when mom undid my safety belt and nudged me out of the front seat. We'd parked in the dead grass in the front yard of what looked like a haunted house. The outline was three stories high and the house looked like an old, run-down Victorian lady. In her day, high society would visit and have tea and biscuits with her owners, but not now. Shadowy strangers lingered around the front yard in between a bunch of cars parked haphazardly all over the lawn. A couple stood kissing on the front steps, oblivious to their surroundings. Loud music, laughter, and shouting came from behind the partially open front door. I smelled smoke from different types of cigarettes, and I didn't see any other children.

"Hey, darlin'!" My mom yelled at one of the figures on the front lawn as she sashayed 10 feet ahead of me. I stood right where she left me when she let go of my hand, and wondered if I should get back in the car. I saw the figure, a man, embrace her and kiss her cheek while they lingered together for a few seconds. I didn't know him. I stayed put, feeling more and more confused and a little frightened.

Why is everything so dark? I wondered. *Are the grown-ups trying to hide from each other? Where are the kids that I can play with?*

Mom ran back to me and led me inside. The smoke was even stronger inside the house, and the sights, sounds, and smells that hit me nearly knocked me on my behind. I gripped Mom's hand even tighter as grown-ups huddled around me.

I became very scared.

"Mommy!" I squeaked, pulling desperately on her hand. All I saw was her hand and forearm in front of me.

DETACHED

"Well, look who we have here! Aren't you precious?" said a curvy blonde woman as she leaned over to stroke my hair and smile at me. A fake smile. Her eyes weren't at all wrinkly, and I pulled away as she closed in. She smoked cigarettes like mom did and curved her pursed lips to the side so she wouldn't blow smoke in my face.

"Marty, come here, look at this tiny little angel! What's your name, pumpkin?" the curvy blonde woman asked as she straightened herself upright. I squeezed Mom's hand even tighter, but she remained invisible past her forearm and I nearly lost my grip as more and more grown-ups drew near.

I stayed silent. Mommy always told me to never speak to strangers. I ducked down and maneuvered my body through the sea of legs until I saw Mom's dress. In an instant, I was hanging on to her leg for dear life.

"Mommy! I'm scared!" I cried, and it caught her attention for the instant I needed it to.

"Sweetheart, these are Mommy's friends! You don't have to be scared," she reassured me as she lifted me up and held me so we were face-to-face. She held me tightly and smiled a real smile before announcing to the crowd, "Hey, everyone, this is my baby girl Bridgette, and she's here to make sure all of you behave like all good people should! She's going to look after you, but you need to look after her, too!"

Mom carried me to the living room couch and set me on its back where I could lean against the wall and set my feet on a big throw pillow on the couch seat. My anxiety dropped a little, because from here, I felt like the tallest person in the room and that I could see everyone around me.

As time passed, more grown-ups came and went, and Mom made her way from room to room, visiting with strangers, hugging others, and finally settling on the man from the front yard that she danced with for a long time. The smoke, all of it in whatever form, made my eyes water and I closed them to block out the irritation. I just wanted to go home.

And I fell asleep for I don't know how long.

When I awoke, I was curled up in the corner of the couch with a blanket tossed over me. A woman—not my mom—lay foot to foot with me on the other two-thirds of the couch. The room was dark, save for one light that beamed in from the hallway, and I heard distant, muffled, indistinct sounds coming from other rooms in the house. There was no more music, no more dancing, and six passed-out adults in the living room with me.

One of them was my mother, whom I found curled up on a chaise lounge four feet from where I'd slept.

"Mommy, Mommy, wake up!" I whispered as I pulled on her sleeve. She swatted the disturbance away as if it was a bothersome gnat.

"Mom, wake up! I want to go home!" I cried, more loudly this time.

She stirred and opened her eye . . .unforgiving. . .impaired.

"Wha, what? Who. . .Bridgette? What are you doing here?" she asked, confused. "You should be in bed! What time is it?"

"Mommy, I don't know how to get home. We're in some scary house and there are people all around," I said.

She sat up as if electrocuted.

"Come on, Bridgette, we have to go home now. I'm sorry, honey. Don't be scared. . .we've had an adventure, right? Remember the fireworks last night? And we had really yummy food for dinner? Remember that?" Her voice was shrill.

Frantic.

§

Years later when I reflected on this July 4th outing, I realized that, in some small way, my mother was trying her best to take care of me. At least I could identify her reasoning, flawed though it was. To her young mind, the worst-case scenario was that she would leave a four-year-old at home all alone while she attended a party in the bad part of town. Bringing me with her was a lesser form of abandonment, a lesser form of what is now known as child endangerment. And it was the first of many times I would be dragged into a world of debauchery as an innocent witness who would grow up too fast, too soon, and without understanding that my world wasn't the same as every other child's world.

My mother was a single, twenty-one-year-old parent with a four-year-old daughter. She'd missed out on all the high school activities, proms, and young adult activities and milestones that her peers enjoyed. She dropped out of high school, so college was obviously out of the question for so many reasons. Maybe her partygoing was an attempt to make up for lost time. Maybe she was trying to escape. Maybe she even had a death wish. The complicated relationship between her and her own mother was, at its very core, the epitome of a love-hate, life-and-death, forgiving-and-unforgiving tug-of-war that never really settled into acceptance, forgiveness, and love. Maybe that was the reason for everything.

And a once witty, beautiful, inspired, and talented young woman spiraled from a life filled with hopes and dreams into a young woman who'd aged exponentially from the burdens of the realities of her choices. A young woman who, by the time she was twenty-five years old, was an emotionally and physically crippled prisoner to her demons—both real and imagined—with little to no thought for the innocent child standing by who desperately wanted to save her.

CHAPTER 5

The Wonder Years

"Mom, it'll be OK. I'll just be a few hours away! I'll probably see you more now than I have all through high school!" Tye said recently, on the heels of his journey to college.

"Oh Tye, honey, I know. It's just a bittersweet time. Let me be happy and sad, OK?" I sighed as my voice broke. I looked away as the tears started and gave him a big hug.

"Aww Mom. Don't cry. At least now you don't have to deal with my dirty socks!" He laughed as he hugged me tighter.

This turning point in my eldest son's life brought back a flurry of memories and a life-flashed-before-my-eyes recap of the events surrounding my own college years. My granddad had long passed, and my mother and grandma didn't share the same emotions that I was now going through with my oldest.

My college experience was one of drive, ambition, and focus. I would do everything I could to better myself and remove myself from a childhood that had been so challenging. All the energy I had was laser-pointed toward my goal of finishing college as soon as I possibly could so I could make a brand-new life for myself and move far, far away from the only life I ever knew.

Tye's experience—or rather, the impending *verge* of his experience—was much more ordinary, much more common, and much less intense than mine. While I knew he was nervous about the transition, he was also really excited and looked forward to his first time really away from home and for the new friends and experiences along the way.

Looking back and looking forward, I'm glad to say I broke the cycle of madness.

§

My biological birthday was June 3rd, and while the fourth of July is America's birthday, it also marks the date when I was baptized at one-month-old. So, in my family, it's when I was really "born."

You sometimes hear people declare that nothing was anything until the day they were baptized, that they were "nothing" or "unsaved" until that day. Since I was a newborn when I was baptized, I grew up thinking that it was my actual birthday, just a month after my real birthday.

In a similar metaphor of biological versus actual, St. Mark's School became my first home, really. It was a community where I felt protected and loved. Safe. Secure. It was a small, private, Catholic school and the teachers and the friends who surrounded me there were very nurturing and loving. The teachers were very strict, but that was exactly the security and regimented environment that I needed in my life, and I felt good being at St. Mark's. It was my family.

But every day when it got closer to three o'clock, my anxiety rose, because I never knew from day to day what would happen when school let out. I didn't know if I would go to my mom's apartment, or to my grandparents' house. Would my mother pick me up, or would Granddad? If I went to my grandparents' house, would I stay overnight, or would my mother come to fetch me before bedtime?

I didn't know if my mother would show up drunk, stoned, both, or fully sober. Would she take me straight home, or to some party? Would it only be one party or a "party hop" night? It was just always the unknown.

"Bridgette, get in the car. Hurry up!" Mom snapped. She wasn't wearing makeup, so I knew she was really rushed. But apparently not so rushed to pick me up. She was nearly three hours late and it was getting dark. Cigarette smoke billowed from the newly opened passenger window, cracked just an inch or two. When Mom smoked in the car—any car—the windows were always shut tight. It's as if she wanted to save all the smoke she could... as if she wanted to immerse herself in the nicotine high and absorb all of it by osmosis.

She was in a car that I didn't recognize, and for once I felt truly angry. I was furious that I lost all that time waiting for her, that I was unable to do my homework and that my whole body was tense just scrutinizing every car that turned the corner. For three hours.

"Where are we going? Where have you been?" I asked. I didn't move an inch from where I stood.

I'd never pushed back before, but I was so tired of this ongoing anxiety. *No child should be put through this*, I thought. *I should be riding my bike around the neighborhood and playing Barbies at my friends' houses, or having them come over to mine and chow down on apples and ants on a log. Why can't I just have a normal life?*

"Young lady, do as I ask. I don't have time for any back talk! Get. In. The. Car," Mom ordered, with a firmer voice this time, and a look that all mothers know and use: *Don't make me get out of this car.*

"I need to be with Granddad tonight. I need help with my math homework," I retorted, still planted firmly where I stood. *Do not give in*, I thought as I dug my heels into the grass.

"Bridgette Allan, get in the car this minute or you're in for some trouble!" she shrieked.

I felt a pang of fear and got in the car. Mom rarely showed anger toward me, and I didn't know how to react, so I followed her orders. She'd never ever taken a hand to me, but I didn't want to push it, either. When I slammed the door shut, she took off like a bullet and didn't say a word to me the rest of the night. It was the scariest feeling to get in the car with her. . .a very uneasy, scary, anxious feeling. I didn't know whose car we were in, who I would meet once we got home, if we would get home, or if we would even get to our destination alive.

She pulled astride the curb in front of our dark apartment and honked the horn. Almost instantly, the living room light popped on and the front door opened. A man I didn't know came out and walked toward the driver side of the car as Mom and I got out. He walked around the back of the car to avoid any contact with me.

DETACHED

"Bridgette, go inside and lock the door. I'll be home late," my mom said.

"But who is that man? Where are you going? What time is 'late'? Who's going to take me to school tomorrow?" I asked. The questions followed one right after the other.

"Just go inside" was all I got in return.

And as with many nights, I didn't see my mother until the next day. I quickly learned to stop asking questions and was just glad to see her, no matter what her condition. At least she was home.

And alive.

I always wanted to have friends come over after school or on weekends, but I was so very embarrassed. Embarrassed by my mother's addictions and how she would act. Embarrassed by the filthy surroundings my grandparents lived in. Nothing about my life was normal, and I never wanted my friends to see how I actually lived, especially when they all lived in such different . . . such *opposite* conditions. When I was at school, I was just Bridgette. Everything was normal. I wasn't judged because of my family or where I lived.

I think when most kids are young, from kindergarten-age up to maybe fifth or sixth grade, they don't remember much. Elementary school is usually a blur and, unless you break an arm or witness something spectacular, such as a moon landing that everyone makes a fuss over, memories don't usually form during those years. Maybe you'll remember your first beloved teacher or a first crush or your first pet, but not much more.

My life, however, was not normal, and I didn't fall into the glut of kids my age who didn't have memories. My earliest memories started at the age of four. And by the time I was six years old, I'd already lived a life that I knew was unique. Different. Stunted, in a way. None of my friends had my life. And I knew they would never want my life. I didn't want it. But I kept plowing through school and did the best I could to always excel, no matter the challenges I faced at home.

By the time I turned ten years old, I was already grown up. I looked after my mother as best I could, and I always had an "A" average in school. I never told anyone about my life out of school, even though it was getting harder to cope. Mom was, by this time, chronically drunk and under the influence of many substances, which left me in a state of constant anxiety for her health and life. I never knew what I would come home to, whether she'd be sober, passed out, or outright dead. She'd long ago stopped picking me up from school, and I always expected the worst when my grandparents fetched me.

One day, I noticed the bulletin board in the school's main hallway pinned with a flyer for Al-Anon, for children of alcoholics. Granddad drove me to the meetings a few times each week, and they made me feel really good. I found it so helpful to talk to other kids whose parents were alcoholics, but I could never, ever let my mom know that I was attending these meetings. She would never let me go back to my grandparents' house if she knew Granddad was taking me to the meetings. Thankfully, she never found out.

"Hi. My name is Annie. What's your name?" asked a girl at my third meeting.

"I'm Bridgette," I replied. I was a little anxious, but not scared. I knew I was among friends.

"My dad is an alcoholic and my parents are getting a divorce," Annie began. "He blacks out. I know my mom loves him, but he makes her cry almost every day and she says she can't stand it anymore."

"Where do you live?" I asked. I was still very hesitant to reveal much at such an early time.

"Oh, we live in Cheltenham. It's just my brother and me. We have a dog named Charlie. Do you have any pets?" Annie asked.

I told her about my old pet ferret and my cat, then backed off a little. I would eventually get to know Annie and the other kids a lot better over the next few days and weeks, but after I discovered that many of the kids were from well-to-do families who lived in nice areas of PG County, it set me on my butt. I kind of always thought alcoholism and substance abuse were conditions suffered by those who lived in the inner city or those who were uneducated or "bad." Attending these meetings really opened my eyes to the fact that addiction can happen to anyone of any age, sex, religion, and socioeconomic background. Addiction doesn't discriminate. I learned so much about the illness that I wrote every single class report on it. All my teachers knew about my situation and yes, I survived it, but I built walls that still stand around me to this day. But in those early years, I learned to *not* feel emotions. I pushed them down and ignored them. I might have felt sad inside, but I never, ever let on that I was anything but happy and well adjusted. I stayed numb. And to this day, I can't be a Debbie Downer. I never wanted to be "that person," because everything she represents is just so unattractive to me.

So the person I wanted to be, the happy, well-adjusted, positive person, is the person I was and am to this day. My friends and even my kids' friends confide in me a lot. I'm so humbled by it. I feel honored that they trust me with their thoughts, fears, and triumphs, and I love that they've chosen me to share their thoughts with. It is one of the things in my life that I'm most proud of.

As I grew to my very early teens, the stress increased. I never knew if my mom's boyfriend would be around or whether he would beat her up or even kill her. Add to that the anxiety of my daily school routine and now the expectations that older kids had for weekend activities. I absolutely hated weekends more than anything else because I never knew what to expect at home. I loved it when my friends had sleepovers or birthday parties because I could just escape from my life. From my own brutal reality.

I loved going to my friends' homes, because they all came from normal, middle-class families. That's all I wanted for my life. Normalcy. Family dinners and watching *Wheel of Fortune* afterward. Taking a glorious hot shower with the lights turned on and feeling the warmth of the water beating down on my skin. Reaching for a lush Turkish towel to dry off and crawling into a real bed with crisp, clean sheets. Waking up to feel the warmth of a fireplace in the winter and eating home-cooked food. Whatever you'd see in a Norman Rockwell painting is what I wanted for my life. And for my mother's life.

"Bridgette, get in the car. Hurry up!" my mom squealed. This time, I was excited to get in because my mom grinned from ear to ear and motioned excitedly for me to hop in.

"Mom, where are we going? Whose car is this?" I asked.

"Oh sweetheart, let's just go for a ride! I got this from the dealership! They're letting me take it for a test drive. Wanna do some donuts?"

We drove to the empty school parking lot and she put me in her lap, stomped on the gas pedal, and swung the steering wheel all the way left. The car lurched into a tight circle and I smelled the rubber tires smoke through the closed windows. Her cigarette smoke was a welcome diversion.

"Wooo hooo!" Mom cried, giggling so hard that her spasming belly tickled my back.

I wanted life to be like this all the time. Just Mom and me, laughing and living. Together.

But since that ideal life would never happen, I found some solace with my pets. We had to give away my ferret because it attacked the neighbor's baby during a visit. Ferrets love milk, and the baby was freshly fed. A little nibbling ensued and the baby's parents threatened to call animal control until my mom promised to rehome my poor little ferret.

She knew I was devastated, and replaced him with a ginger cat, Tinker, whom she loved as much as I did. He lived in our apartment and was the apple of my eye. He would greet me when I got home from school or my grandparents' house and follow me into my room. He'd sleep with me every night and would be there whenever I felt sad or scared.

He also had a little bed in one of my dresser drawers that he liked to hang out in. I put a blanket in it, and when he got tired of being near me, that's where he'd go. I just wanted him next to me all the time, though, when I was watching TV, doing my homework, or reading. But cats aren't like dogs. He was very independent and I wanted to control him, to keep him near me. He was the only thing I could control in my life, really. He was my support. There were many nights when I'd cry myself to sleep, cry into his soft fur as he purred near my face. Tinker was the being that kept me sane in that apartment.

Deep down, my mom was a very caring, very proper woman who had an inborn sense of decency and honor. She was always made up and her hair perfect whenever she left the house. She took pride in her appearance, and anyone looking at her wouldn't ever guess what went on behind closed doors. Even inside, no one would ever find traces of her addiction. I certainly never did. The most anyone could say was that she wasn't the best housekeeper. And at heart, her biggest heartbreak was that she was never truly deeply loved by a man. She craved the love of a man. Of a good man. And I would see her with all these abusive men, these "boyfriends," and I'd ask myself, why on earth would you love a man that does that to you? Why do you even need a man?

Of course, I didn't understand it back then. I just saw it as such weakness. Why was she too weak to leave a man who abused her? Why was she too weak to stand up for herself and not let somebody treat her that way? The situation was just mind boggling, both then and now. And all these years later, the questions remain unanswered.

These men had nothing to offer at all. I would imagine at the very start and shortly into a new relationship there was always hope, that maybe this man would be the one, the knight in shining armor. I think even when things got bad, there was still that little girl hope in Mom's mind and in her heart. She'd tell me sometimes that "He's not that horrible. And he was so nice at the beginning." And later, after the abuse, "Well, he's sorry, you know, he's just really upset and stressed out from work, but he's really sorry. He promised he'd never do it again."

And she always forgave the men, to the exclusion and denial of her own feelings. And when she denied herself for so long, she would eventually act out.

"Sweetheart," mom yelled from the kitchen. "Get ready. We're going to Bill's company picnic."

Bill was mom's longtime boyfriend. He was a plumber who'd worked for the same company for years and made a decent salary as long as he was sober. Bill was also the only man who nearly killed my mother on more than one occasion. And yet, she hung on for dear life.

And even though Mom tried to convince my twelve-year-old self that this carnival-style picnic would have rides and games and carnival food, I was still loath to go because I knew there would be a beer truck present. My mother always attended parties that had a beer truck. I tried every way to get out of it, but she was insistent that I go.

To make matters worse, she snagged my black spandex biking shorts and a fitted tank top. It was perfect for its purpose, working out, but not as something you'd wear at a family picnic. It was a very hot day and Mom still wore the outfit because it was so tight and revealing, in its own way. Nothing disgusting or X-rated, but just...inappropriate. I was mortified and didn't want to be seen with her. Other moms wore jeans and peasant blouses or sundresses with pretty sandals. *Why couldn't my mom be normal, just for once?*

Once we got to the picnic, Mom started drinking one beer after another, as if the wellspring would dry up. And she got very surly very fast. I don't know if it was the combination of endless free beer on a hot day or if she was just in a mood, but the day was hellish.

I always did my best to eat as healthily as I could and was always active. But on this day, the beer taunted my mother and fresh, hot, thick-cut French fries taunted *me*. They called to me even more than the attention of a handsome boy nearby who'd been stealing glances with me and smiling.

"Mom, can we get some French fries?" I asked quietly. I didn't want him to know I wanted fries. I didn't want to spoil the image. It's similar to when you're in a new relationship and have to *really* go to the bathroom for the first time. You're mortified because women aren't supposed to do that! Everything is supposed to be perfect and sweet and not. . .human. It's the silliest thing, really, but that's how I felt. It's how all teenagers all over the world feel at that age. Everything is changing in their bodies and lives and even the tiniest things are upsetting.

"Wait, what? You want some FRIES, Bridgette?" my mother bellowed at the top of her voice. I wanted to crawl in a hole and die right there. It was as loud and as cringeworthy as the scene in *Bridesmaids* where Annie Walker takes a sedative on an airplane and starts screaming and taunting passengers and the flight crew.

"Well, Mom, I was thinking we could share them?" I said meekly, but loudly enough so people immediately surrounding us could hear. Including the smiling boy.

DETACHED

"Bridgette, just order the damned fries. Oh, where is my purse? BILL! Where's my purse? Oh hi there, can I have another beer? Thank you. Oh, my shoe. There's a stone or something in it. . .ow. Bridgette, what are you still doing here? I thought you wanted some fries! Go get them, for crying out loud!"

"I don't want them now. I'm not hungry anymore. I just thought you might like to share them because you haven't had anything to eat today and. . .you really should eat something because I don't want you to pass out," I said as I died a little more with each passing second.

"Oh GEEZ little girl! Just go get the damned fries! What's the big deal! If you want them, you said you wanted them, just GO GET THEM!" By this time, she was all-out shrieking and spilling her beer and Bill was embarrassed, the smiling boy disappeared, and everyone within earshot was backing off. Other moms shuffled their kids away from the scene and over to quieter pastures and Mom was left drunk, out of breath, and furious.

I just started crying. I couldn't stop. She huffed and stomped over to the fry guy and ordered the biggest plate of fries and threw them on the table in front of me.

"Go ahead! There are your fries, Bridgette!" she slurred. "Stop acting like a little BITCH."

I looked at my mother with disbelief. I'd never witnessed an outburst like this. She'd never lashed out at me, ever, much less called me bad names. She wasn't crying, but her mascara was running and her lipstick smeared. The beer in her cup spilled all over the grass as she tried to steady herself. Even Bill was shocked at her behavior.

We drove home in silence, and Mom and Bill had a huge fight when we got home. I ran into my room and cried for a few hours. Even with Tinker at my side, I was inconsolable.

The situation just got worse and worse. The final nail in the coffin happened at the time of the annual Preakness horse race. I was at my grandparents' house because my mom and her sister, Rose, went to enjoy the race and the parties. They ended up in a place called "The Pit," which was the place where attendees gather to drink. All day long. And The Pit wasn't like some ritzy, country club gathering, it was muddy and messy and filled with rowdy, drunk people.

Granddad always liked watching the news, and on that day, heard the newscaster mention the Preakness race. We both perked up to see which horse won.

But the news story had nothing to do with the winner. It instead focused on two women running along the tops of the porta-potties and one of them setting a fire before engaging in a full-on brawl with the other woman.

Wow, I thought. *Mom would kill me if I ever did that.*

"Come on, Bridge," said my granddad. "Let's have dinner. Come on, now. Enough of that."

Just as we finished dinner, there was a commotion outside and my grandmother looked out the front window to check it out.

"What's the noise?" I asked.

"Oh nothing, child. Just put the dishes in the sink and settle down," my grandmother ordered.

I noticed the look she gave Granddad, and we both went running for the door.

And when I opened it to look outside, all I saw was my mother lying on the front lawn passed out.

She looked dead.

"Mom! Mommy! Wake up!" I cried as I bent over her to see if she was still breathing.

"Huh, what? Oh Bridgette...can you go get my hairbrush? I need my hairbrush. Where is it?" she asked. She was completely drunk, and it was then that I noticed the blood on her shirt.

I realized that she was one of the porta-potty women.

"Mom, what is the matter with you? Why are you doing this to us? Why are you acting like... such a baby?!?" I cried as I ran back into the house and locked the door behind me.

I think eventually Bill picked her up because she was gone in the morning when I left for school.

I knew that people did stupid things, irrational things, childish things...and that forgiveness was a virtue. And sure, Mom had no young adulthood because she became a mother at such a young age, and maybe she was making up for lost time. But her actions still had me wondering what was wrong with her. None of my friends' mothers acted like this; they didn't end up as embarrassing objects of news fodder. It was one thing for her to misbehave and lose control at home, but bringing her irresponsible actions out into public was another thing altogether. It's not what proper people did, and I realized that even though I was only twelve. I don't blame her for her actions, because looking back, I know she was sick and that she suffered anguish that none of us will ever understand or come face-to-face with. But as a child, I remember thinking that she should have been more responsible, that she should have gone to college, that she should have had her life together already. But no. Instead, she was passed out on the front lawn after getting into a catfight with another grown woman and setting structures on fire before being called out on the local news as an agitator.

And that very night, I decided to take control of my own life. I had to think about high school, where I would go to high school, and how I would transition from St. Mark's as smoothly as I could. My safe place, school, was about to change and I didn't know if it was for the better or for the worse.

I love my mother and always have, but on that night, as a grown-up-too-soon twelve-year-old, I swore I would never repeat the cycle, that my life would be very different than hers. I would be responsible for my own destiny and take care of my loved ones in ways she couldn't comprehend or manage.

My life was up to me.

CHAPTER 6

A Family, Deconstructed

I'm sure I'm not the only kid who came from a family with an absentee dad and a mom who struggled with her own problems: nonexistent self-esteem, problems with abusive relationships, and substance abuse among them.

And it's a result of this environment that, to this day, I still harbor fear, anxiety, and shame. I consider them my weaknesses. Old habits—and conditioning—die hard. Because of the life she lived and the choices she made, there was very little left of my mother emotionally to use those reserves to love me. I know she loved me, deep down, but not in the all-American stereotypical mom way. Not in the way a mom would lift a car off her child or throw herself in front of an attacker to save her children. At least I don't think so. She was so busy trying to keep herself afloat—and alive—that her struggle was all-consuming and in its own way, self-centered. Narcissistic. There was no room for anyone else.

My granddad had a huge influence on me. He was like my mother, father, best friend, and mentor all rolled into one. Everyone should be as lucky as I was—and am. Because of his love, I developed self-esteem, a go-get-'em attitude, resilience, and strength. He taught me proper manners, good sportsmanship, and how to manage life as a child and as an adult. Granddad used to help me make peanut butter and jelly sandwiches for all six of my Cabbage Patch Kids dolls. Each and every one. We would sit outside at the picnic table in the front yard with all of the dolls and have lunch.

"You see, sweetheart, making sandwiches is a very special talent," Granddad said the first time we had a picnic. He whispered it in my ear as if it was a secret.

"First you have to have all your ingredients and tools in place . . ." he explained. "The French, who are great chefs, call it a meesun plass." He meant *mise en place*, but I was too young to know how to spell that!

Granddad laid out a tablecloth and on it, a jar of peanut butter, a jar of grape jelly, two knives, a bread knife, eight paper plates, eight napkins, and a couple of damp paper towels folded in half.

The lesson began.

"You need to work on this like an assembly line. I'll show you."

I sat mesmerized. It was as if magic was about to happen.

"First, you have to line up the bread. . . four slices in a square," he started. I sat next to him on the little picnic bench with my dolls lined up watching us.

"Then what?" I asked eagerly.

"Well, next comes the peanut butter. You always have to have three knives: one for the peanut butter, one for the jelly, and one for cutting the sandwiches. Each knife has its special purpose." Granddad nudged me and laughed.

He then proceeded to use one knife to dip into the peanut butter jar and carefully spread some on two of the bread slices, working it to the very edges of the bread. I got to lick the knife, and he motioned to the paper towels when I was through.

"Always clean up after yourself. It's the proper thing to do, it's good manners," he urged.

Next came the jelly. It was a new jar of Concord grape jelly, and I watched as Granddad opened the jar with a swift twist and heard the gentle "pop" as the seal broke. He grabbed the second knife and stuck it into the jelly as he stirred for a few seconds.

When he withdrew the knife, the jelly looked like deep amethyst caviar. He spread it on top of the peanut butter and left a little edge so it wouldn't overflow.

"Grape jelly stains, honey. That's why you leave a little border all around."

I nodded. A little border. Got it.

Then he topped the sandwich with the top slice and trimmed off the crusts. Then he cut each of the two sandwiches into four neat triangles. Two triangles went on my plate, and one triangle landed on the little plates in front of my six dolls.

"But Granddad, what about you? Aren't you going to eat?"

"Honey, don't you worry about me. I'll have something later!"

I thought my dolls were all such great little eaters. But rather, it was Granddad who would secretly eat all the sandwiches. I don't think he minded at all! He was great at playing make-believe with me, but there was always a lesson to be learned. We always said our prayers before each meal and always put our napkins on our laps. We said "please" and "thank you" the way polite people do, and we always took our dishes to the sink. Granddad would wipe my dolls' tiny mouths in case the jelly got a little messy. It was a great primer for life.

I don't think I ever heard Granddad speak negatively about anything or anyone. He was the most positive person I knew, and I now know where my mom got her optimism, even in her devastating state of life. Even when Granddad grew frail and started losing his hair from the cancer, he remained full of strength, dignity, and confidence. "I'm always grateful for another beautiful day on this Earth," he would say, his eyes twinkling, and his never-give-up attitude and positivity rubbed off on me. I rarely ever saw the point in complaining. I never understood the "glass is half empty" mentality. The naysayers were weak, in my opinion. And that's because Granddad was so strong. But after he died at the too-young age of fifty-nine years old, just as I started high school in 1990, I felt I was flying aimlessly through the sky—untethered to anything safe and stable.

But the one thing he couldn't impart on me. . . was a role he could never fill. While he surely helped to fill most of the emotional holes that my mother had emotionally and psychically pierced in me, there was room left that he was unequipped to replenish.

And it's something I couldn't turn to my stricken mother or grandmother for, this relationship that most girls take for granted. They were so busy dealing with their own tangled lives that there was no room for me.

With the failure of these two traditionally closest female relationships, what I needed was girls and women in my life who weren't broken, who didn't hate themselves, who didn't take abuse from others or dish it out mercilessly. I needed that mom, that aunt, that older sister, and a BFF. Or three.

As much as I excelled in my studies and had friends in school, I was still reserved. I was used to making myself as small as possible—both physically and emotionally—when I was in my mother's home. I shut off and never invited friends over. It was less suffocating in my grandparents' home because at least there, I knew my grandfather was a shining light.

One of the many things he taught me was the importance of striving for higher goals, even if you never imagined you could achieve them, which made me realize I had to expand my world. All work and no play and all of that. So in a 180...no...a 360-degree somersault, I joined the cheerleading squad. I'd been a cheerleader in middle school at St. Mark's, but high school was way different. These were the big leagues, especially to a teenager. Starting in ninth grade, I made the squad and cheered for two years with Sharon, who was in tenth grade, and Brooke and Jessica, who were in eleventh grade. I knew Sharon and Jessica since kindergarten. We all went to St. Mark's together. However, we became closer in middle school.

There's nothing small, reserved, or shy about cheerleaders. And of course, there are girls who fuel the stereotype of jock-dating, superficial "mean girls" who bully anyone who didn't make the team or people who are less than Ken and Barbie attractive. Sometimes they're even thought of as snobby and even trampy.

But in reality, all the girls on our squad didn't even come close to those misconceptions. We all came from different backgrounds. I was an only child, but the rest of the squad's members had siblings. Some were more affluent than others, but one thing we all had in common was that we were determined to have good, successful lives.

Each and every one of them was kind, generous, and well-liked by everyone—our teachers, the students, and the athletes. With and because of them, I flourished. In the days before helicoptering political correctness became the norm, the "black" girls called us the "white girls." It was all in good humor, and we were well respected among our peers, especially the basketball players. They brought us into their group and vice versa. Racial differences only brought us closer together and taught us to be accepting and nonjudgmental. It was the meaning of true friendship and helped us realize that at the end of the day, we were all just human beings trying to make it in this world. Trying to escape our own set of circumstances. We all looked out for each other and would go to bat for each other at a moment's notice.

Cheerleading helped me to find order in an otherwise disorderly world and home life. While my mother could be erratic, one moment erupting with anger over a tiny misstep and the next embracing me tearfully, remorseful over her actions or reactions, cheerleading served to give me structure. Its formations, direct, scripted cheers, choreography, and the goal of reaching perfection in our routines helped me find a transformative, safe space to be. One way we depended on each other came when we did basket tosses or a raised arabesque.

When the "flyer" would be tossed down, she had to depend on the others (the "bases") to catch her. We would never let anyone fall. We would dive underneath their bodies before we would ever let them hit the ground. It was the true meaning of team: *Trust*.

If any of the girls on our team experienced troubles such as mine in their lives, no one knew it. We spent a lot of time at practice, competitions, and in live performance at games. We traveled by bus or car to "away" games and saw each other all dolled up for game day as well as unadorned and zit-ridden when we were down. But none of that mattered. Not only were we a team, we grew as close as any family related by blood. We confided in each other about boys, sex, getting our periods, and the tough neighborhoods that some of us lived in. We trusted, knowing that there would never be any judgment. And there never was. Within this group of young women, I learned what life could be like if you put yourself "out there."

I got a taste of what it was like to be expansive—to branch out past the dark confines of my attic bedroom. To step out of the safe space in my mother's apartment, past the land mines that separated it from the front door. To mentally and emotionally risk pain, rejection, and judgment only to find a true family.

Three girls on the squad, in particular, quickly became—and remain—my closest friends to this day: Brooke, Jessica, and Sharon. We began cheering together in high school. During my runaway adventure, I stayed with their families and they were the first people other than my grandfather to show me the meaning of acceptance, respect, and love.

All of them came from average, middle-class families. Brooke's parents were divorced and her mom struggled a little to make ends meet from time to time, but that didn't keep her from being a rock-solid head of the family. Jessica and Sharon both had strong families with both parents heading up their households. Their siblings were not only smart and educated, but athletic, too. Their families were very "Leave it to Beaver" solid, supportive, non-dysfunctional, with dinner on the table by 6:00 p.m. every night.

Brooke was two years older than me. She was sassy and sophisticated. . .a cute little bombshell with long, perfectly curled blonde hair. Her lipstick was always flawless and her mascara precisely defined every long eyelash. She wore Daisy Duke jean shorts and ruffled tops with sandals that showed off her figure and manicured toes. Brooke wore the tiniest cross-body purses that could barely contain a lipstick, a pager, and some mad money. She reminded me of a mix between Alicia Silverstone and Reese Witherspoon: savvy and fashionable with a ton of spunk. All the girls wanted to be in her circle of friends and all the guys wanted to ask her out but were terrified. But this was her mojo. It was her thing. And it worked. I was instantly drawn to her.

She was like a big sister. When I was in eighth grade before we "officially" met, I was dating Steve, a senior, and showed up at the prom as dolled up as I could be. It was awkward, to say the least. You're not quite in high school and are usually thought of as invisible. Plus, at that age, dating someone four years older represented a huge span not only in age, but also in experience, school relationships, goals, and expectations. Steve was the kindest young man with the biggest heart. He was a gentle giant: a big, strong football player who downed four grilled cheese sandwiches after a game and gave me his letterman jacket. I felt on top of the world. He had zero reservations about asking me to the prom and was confident and self-assured, but not conceited. These traits were rare in a "jock" and they were very attractive to me. His family was so supportive of us. I think they knew I was an old soul, but they knew I needed him in an emotional sense. I had never been to such a fancy party and it must have showed from a mile away. One of Steve's friends overheard Brooke ask, "Hey, who's the eighth grader over there?" Steve was unfazed. He was a happy-go-lucky type who never worried about what others thought. He definitely marched to the beat of his own drum.

While most girls might have heckled or criticized me, Brooke didn't, even though she was a sophomore. After a few sneaky side-glances and some snide remarks, she apparently decided that we were meant to be new, fast friends. She slowly made her way over to me—out of curiosity at first. It only took a short time to figure out that we had more in common than Brooke had hoped. She took me under her wing. And for a popular high school kid to do that just proved how mature and generous she was.

Of my three "sisters by other mothers," Brooke was the fun one. She and I were totally into long "pageant hair" that was popular in the 1990s like you saw in the Miss USA pageants. We loved to dance, we loved trendy fashions, and just loved each other's company. Our life paths continued to mirror each other, as we both competed in beauty pageants and went on to become professional NFL and NBA cheerleaders. She taught me that everyone has stories of survival. We both traveled the country and the world in search of our dreams, which were, when we met, simply to get out of Prince George's County. We shared the goal of getting through college and moving on in life. Our cheerleading continued in college, where we both dated older guys and athletes and attended the most sought-after sophisticated parties. We really were the "in" crowd but at the same time we never fit the behavioral "mold" of traditional cheerleaders. But I will admit to this: we *did* love keeping fit, eating healthy, and never leaving our homes without being impeccably coiffed, dressed, and perfumed up.

Jessica was also a sophomore, but was more like a big sister and a mom rolled into one. She was always full of words of wisdom and just seemed to "get it." She knew where I came from. She knew my circumstances. She knew I'd been in survival mode for most of my life and always advised me to ignore what other people thought. "Don't even worry about it!" she'd say. "It's none of their business. You do you." Jessica taught me never to be swayed by anyone's opinions. She believed in me *and* my decisions, even when they seemed "off the beaten path."

Jessica had the most beautiful, warm smile that could light up a room. People were instantly drawn to her infectious smile and positive attitude. She always gave the best hugs and took care to be protective of me. Jessica was the one who taught me how to drive in my grandmother's old white station wagon when I was fourteen. The overhead lining inside the car was ripped out, so every few seconds, it felt like it was "snowing" pieces of foam on our heads. The radio didn't work either, so we kept my yellow boom box between us in the front bench seat. We had a popular mix tape playing at all times. Her favorite singer was Mariah Carey, and she was always singing along to "Vision of Love." I always told her she should've been a professional singer because she had such natural talent. By the age of fourteen, I was driving myself to school. Administrators and security thankfully turned a blind eye when they saw me.

Sharon was in the ninth grade, just a year ahead of me. She was a good cheerleader and an incredible athlete, too. Sharon was phenomenal at softball and could throw a better spiral football than most boys. While she had a quieter disposition, she was confident and smart and never gave in to peer pressure. I distinctly remember the times we would ride in the car with her mom, who was also a quiet type. Her mom never gave her grief or asked the difficult questions that I assumed most high school moms asked. Mrs. Battiste trusted Sharon with every ounce of her being and knew that she made the right decisions and didn't have to prove anything to anyone. They had an unspoken understanding that self-respect always came first.

Her family was solid as a rock. She never felt unsafe or unsure. She never had to wonder what would happen next in her life. It was consistent and methodical. Hers was what a real home looked like. Sharon had a huge calendar on her desk in her bedroom and she used to draw a picture of the hairstyle she was going to wear for each day: a ponytail on Monday, a French braid on Tuesday, sides back on Wednesday, and so on. Not only was she extremely organized but she was also a very talented artist. She was a steady, reliable, unwavering friend who was comfortable in her own skin. Sharon taught me that the quietest one in the room is usually the smartest, and that not everything requires your attention or comment. She taught me that flying under the radar was often the best way to go, and was expert at keeping secrets secret. She never depended on affirmations from friends to know who she was inside. As pretty as Sharon was, she never flaunted it. She had beautiful blue eyes and thick, blonde hair. She dressed a little more on the conservative side, but always very stylish.

It's remarkable that our paths crossed at all and that we became friends. When you're that young, you usually stick to friends in your own grade. Even one year's difference makes a big difference in who you hang around with, what your hobbies and activities are, who you ignore, and all the other "class" restrictions that exist, no matter how subtle they are.

I know that's what made our foursome extra special. Here were teenage girls at the very pivot points of their young lives, growing from children to teenagers with all the angst and pent-up hormones and yearnings to fit in . . . anywhere. The maturity that they each possessed by befriending and mentoring me is definitely a rare thing, and I'm blessed that the stars lined up and our paths collided in the best ways possible.

I saw in all three of these unique young women traits that I wanted to emulate. And I wanted to lay bare the truth of my life: the truth about my parents, my mother, just all of it. The shame, the constant anxiety, the devastation over the loss of my grandfather and the different devastation at the loss of my mother. But I'd hidden the truth for my whole life and had no idea how anyone outside of the family would react. Sure, Mrs. Gossart understood and was completely supportive, but she was an adult. I'd never revealed anything so personal to a peer. Or peers.

Until now.

CHAPTER 7

I Want a Divorce

When I reached thirteen, it was the year I became an adult. I didn't have a bat mitzvah; I didn't have a "welcome to your teenage years" party. I didn't get my ears pierced or have a special dinner out with a virgin piña colada to celebrate the transition. I didn't get permission to wear pink lipstick instead of ChapStick or get my first pair of grown-up high heels. At thirteen, I was just trying to survive and fly under the radar.

My mother had me when she was seventeen, just four years older than I was. I couldn't even comprehend what it must have been like to be an unwed teenage mom. She would always tell me, "Kids aren't born with an instruction book!" And I'd remind her, "I don't think you need an instruction book to tell you not to get drunk every night." There were definitely two distinct personalities to my mom: non-sober and sober. She was very much like Dr. Jekyll and Mr. Hyde. When Mom was under the influence, she was not fun to be around. She was not likeable...or funny...she was mean. She called me every name in the book, and more. She belittled me and was condescending. I'm not even sure she liked me. Or herself for that matter.

But when Mom was sober, she was amazing. She was THE BEST EVER. She exuded confidence, poise, stature. She had a presence. She was beautiful and likeable and funny, and everyone wanted to be around her.

That was my mom.

My *sober* mom.

I loved *that* mom.

I craved *that* mom.

My mom would always tell me how difficult it was to be a mother. But she honestly thought she was one of the coolest moms around. One time in elementary school, my mom signed up for recess duty. All of the parents were randomly assigned a day. When I saw her name on the list in my classroom, I remember having anxiety about it for weeks. I was terrified. Would she even show up? I hoped that she would forget. Would she be presentable? Hungover? Dressed appropriately? Would she be able to enforce the classroom rules. . .or would she even try?

Finally, the day arrived. When the clock hit 11:50 a.m., I held my breath and waited.

And waited.

I kept glancing at the door and then the clock. . .11:55, 11:58, 12:00, 12:02.

Each second ticked away as loudly as someone beating a kettle drum next to my ear. I couldn't let my classmates see my anxiety, but my heart was fluttering so hard in my chest that I was certain everyone heard it.

Then the classroom door opened.

In walked the lady with the tight miniskirt and high heels wearing perfume you could smell from across the room. Her hair was perfectly coiffed and sprayed into place and she wore frosted pink lipstick.

My mother.

Oh dear Lord.

There she was. My friends. . .classmates. . .even my teacher stared at her in awe.

Who was *this* woman?

Most of them had never seen her before. To them, especially the girls, she was larger than life.

"Hi everyone! I'm Bridgette's mom!" she said in the loudest voice possible. There wasn't anything quiet about her.

"It looks like rain outside so we will have recess indoors! Who wants to play double Dutch?"

Mom held out jump ropes and dangled them in front of the class.

But as I died a little inside and hoped to crawl in a closet to hide before this got any more embarrassing, my classmates went wild! They thought it was the coolest idea ever and within five minutes of her arrival were jumping rope in the hallway.

How, why, kept running through my head. . .thoughts unanswered in my invisible frenzy. My mom couldn't do this! It was breaking every classroom rule! But these thoughts never crossed her mind. She danced to the beat of her own drum and always decreed that life was about having a good time. Maybe that's where my own confidence comes from.

§

For as long as I can remember, we'd played house hopscotch. Mom and I would leapfrog from one dwelling to another with the same action and reaction: move in with the greatest hope that this would be the last one. That things would work out this time. But as always, the money ran out and we were evicted, then we'd find a new place and camp out there until the next eviction. Lather, rinse, repeat. There was no money to buy furniture or amass any personal belongings other than the clothes on our backs and a few suitcases full of necessities. Still, my mom was optimistic. She always used to tell me, "Think of it, Bridgette, one day we will finally find the house that is truly ours. And then you'll be able to choose just the right color for your walls to match the drapes. One day, one day. . .one day."

My mom went to cosmetology school when I was little, and she would bring me along. It was actually one of my favorite things to do. It felt good to be there with her doing something that we both loved. Beauty and fashion were always a good bonding experience for us. The instructors always let me "help." As a result, my mom became one of the best hairdressers in Washington, D.C., at least for a short period of time. She worked at Pietro's Hair Salon in the Washington Hilton. It was such a prestigious salon and had such sophisticated clientele. She was—and is—a very talented barber, and her clients were always very pleased with her work. My mom's best client wanted her hair French braided for a big event, and Mom was booked solid.

The phone rang and I raced to answer. Ringing phones and knocks on the door always scared me to death. What bad news lay ahead?

"Bridgette," mom whispered excitedly on the phone.

"Mom? Are you OK?" I replied.

"Oh honey, I'm fine. Listen, I need you to come to the salon. Patricia needs a French braid and I'm swamped! I need your help. OK, bye."

I set the receiver back in its cradle in disbelief.

Then I let out a little shriek of excitement.

Wow, me?

I was beyond excited!! And nervous. I wanted to do the best job ever!

I will never forget that day. I walked into the salon...and Mom's client was so excited to let me do her hair. My hands were shaking because I had to live up to her expectations. I proceeded to separate and braid her hair, piece by piece...and fifteen minutes later, my mom's client was in heaven! She loved it! I felt so proud...not only of myself but of my mother who worked in this prestigious salon. I was proud of HER. In fact, because Mom taught me everything she knew, I've actually styled my friends' hair for years.

But alcohol and partying always reared their influence and would result in her getting fired. Time and time again. She could never hold a job for long, and started to rotate salons in the same way patients who become addicted to prescription meds started cycling their way from doctor to doctor when one stops renewing the script. She would always give me an excuse as to why the salon "didn't need her to come in today." And it was just so very sad in so many ways. My mom was talented, beautiful, well dressed, and smelled like Jean Nate perfume. She certainly looked and acted the part. But only for a period of time. Until the drinking took over.

But the day of living in our own home would never come for many more years, and it probably would never come as long as I lived with her.

My entire lifetime was spent watching my mother struggle with substance abuse and the men who abused her, each time knocking her self-esteem down another notch or two. She was constantly in a haze of senses deadened by the demon whiskey and assorted other substances as she tried desperately to maintain who she was. And she thought she would find who she was in the next boyfriend, or the one after that, or the one after that. She would always defend them and somehow blame herself for the abuse they unleashed on her. "Maybe if I was just thinner, or prettier, or if I had nicer things, he'll stop. Or maybe I deserve it," I imagined her thinking as she took the beatings over and over.

Without fighting back.

I'd go to parties with her and sit in the corner while everyone else got drunk and took all manner of drugs. I don't even think it occurred to her that I was a child in a very adult environment. I was just a kid . . . I think I was between five and ten years old during this time. I was so scared that she would get arrested if there was a raid and then I would end up as a foster child somewhere. That was my fear. Even though my living situation with her was not in the least healthy, it was familiar. I could devise a plan to "get out" based on what I already knew. It was a strange feeling of relying on the same patterns of unpredictability. Kind of an oxymoron.

Her life choices and circumstances escalated to the point where I'd find her passed out in the front yard or naked in bed with her brother-in-law or some random guy that we never saw again. Before I learned to drive myself to school at fourteen, I'd miss insane amounts of hours of classes because she was too wasted to drive me to school. Fortunately, my grades were always stellar, so the staff overlooked all that missed time. Looking back, I was more her mother than she was mine.

One of her longest-standing boyfriends, Harold, started out a relatively nice guy, but then turned into a monster who would frequently choke her and beat her senseless. One time he even broke her nose. There was blood everywhere. I got so sick when I saw it—and her—because I thought he'd stabbed her and that she was dying. The abuse happened constantly and it got so bad she'd try to run away from him. He would chase her down the street, catch her, and throw her over the house fence. He was such an evil man that he even tried to kill her a few times. I don't know how she survived. I didn't know what to do to try and save her. If I stepped in to try and help, she might get an even rougher beating. I never stopped to think what could happen to me.

But I would soon find out.

One of the few nights we all had dinner together, Mom cooked frozen vegetables. They were drenched in some sort of sauce that was literally inedible. I have always loved vegetables, but I could not possibly swallow this disgusting marinated vegetable medley. As I moved the food around my plate with my fork, Harold told me I needed to eat all of it.

"Every. Last. Bite, young lady," he barked.

I swear, if I could have forced it down, I would have. But this was not edible. There was zero chance of my plate being cleaned. Zero. I glanced up at the open window where a boom box sat, music bursting from its speakers.

I so wish Mom was drunk right now.

It was the first time I actually wanted my mother to be drunk so she would distract this man. . .this beast whom I was afraid of.

When he told me to clean my plate, I knew he meant it. Fifteen minutes turned into thirty minutes. By the time forty-five minutes passed, I still had not cleaned my plate, and I knew my mother was going to pay for it later.

I got up from the table and walked to my room. As soon as my back was turned, I could hear it. The beating. The screaming. The begging for him to stop.

It wasn't the first time this happened, and when it did, I usually closed my eyes and just hugged my cat. I tried that. I pulled the covers over my head. But this time, I could tell it was bad. Very bad. And it wasn't going away. He wasn't going to stop. This could be the night.

DETACHED

The night that he finally succeeded in killing her.

And as I lay in my bed...listening to my mother cry out in pain...listening to my mother beg him to stop...listening to my mother's pleas...something awakened inside of me. Something innate. Something that was bigger than me.

I jumped out of bed, flung open my bedroom door, and charged into the kitchen. I was ready to confront this lowlife loser with every cell of my body and all the strength I could muster. As I turned the corner and saw my mother crouched on the floor, severely beaten with blood streaming from her eyes, I grew terrified that she was already dead. A kitchen chair lay on its side next to her with one leg broken and the bare bulb above the sink flickered like a weak strobe light, its power draining just as my mother's life force...her spirit...ebbed and flowed. Then weakly and ever so slightly, she lifted her head and turned to me.

And returned her gaze to the floor tiles beneath her broken self.

I charged after Harold.

As I got closer to him, moving in superfast silence, I had no idea what I was going to do when I reached him, but I knew that no matter what, this good-for-nothing piece of trash was not going to get away with this AGAIN. When Harold saw me, he charged right at me, full force, with his eyes ablaze with evil. I'd never seen that look from anyone before or since. I knew he would kill me if he caught me.

I heard my mother whimpering and quickly turned to look at her; the image of her beaten to a pulp, cowering in the corner of the kitchen in a heap on the tiled floor, was almost too much for me to take. And yet, I wondered, for what was probably the hundredth time, why she would stay with this man and subject herself to such pain and torture.

I took a U-turn and ran back into my bedroom with Harold right on my heels. I slammed my door shut and locked the flimsy doorknob lock just as I heard his body hit the door with such force that I thought he'd knock it down and take his anger out on me.

But I didn't care. If I could save my mom from this torment, I'd do it in a minute.

"BRIDGETTE," Harold bellowed as he pounded on the door.

"OPEN THIS DOOR OR I'M GOING TO KNOCK IT RIGHT DOWN!"

As I listened to the waves of sound and room-shuddering impacts happening just a few feet away, I managed to call the local police and quickly tell them what was happening. The dispatcher stayed on the phone with me while I waited for the police to show.

The ten minutes between the time I called and the time cruisers screeched to a stop at our house was the longest ten minutes of my young life.

"I'm scared. I tried to help my mom. . .I don't know what he's going to do," I said to the stranger on the other end.

"It's alright, sweetie," she said in a deeply soothing voice. "The police are on their way right now. Please stay in your room and stay on the line with me, OK? Let me know when you hear the sirens," she assured me. My breathing slowed a little and I kept my eyes closed.

The yelling and pounding stopped and things grew strangely quiet, which scared me more than anything. The dispatcher said something I couldn't understand, then returned to me.

"Help is about a block away," she said. And just as she finished, I heard the sirens.

I'd told the dispatcher everything. I was ready for Harold to get locked up once and for all, and I heard the doorbell followed by loud but muffled words.

"Bridgette," my mother said, in a small, weak voice right outside my door.

"Mom?" I asked, immediately tearing up.

"It's OK, you can come out now," she said.

After about a minute, I slowly opened my door and peered out into the hallway, expecting to see Harold handcuffed on the porch and the police writing up an incident report.

What I saw and then heard rattled me to the core.

Harold was sitting at the kitchen table across from the first policeman. A second officer stood behind Harold and watched as he scribbled on a yellow legal pad.

My mother stood in the hallway a few feet behind the standing officer. Her arms were folded tightly across her chest and every few seconds she'd uncoil to wipe her eyes with a balled-up remnant of tissue.

The officer leaned over to Mom and said something under his breath that I couldn't quite make out. But I heard her response as clear as a bell.

"I don't want to press charges," she said in a voice that was much stronger than the one I'd heard just minutes ago when she summoned me out of my room.

I was in complete disbelief and shock.

WHY was she protecting this monster? What was happening?

For reasons I'll never know, Harold remained in our lives for many more years.

I guess most kids—and even adults—might have wandered into a fantasy world where they imagined a perfect life in a perfect house with a white picket fence and a Honda in the garage. My grandparents' house was infested with cockroaches and we didn't have any heat or running water most of the time. Although my granddad was a genius (by definition) and a successful mechanical engineer as well as a lawyer, the bills never got paid. All the kids drained the family coffers. There were foot-high piles of dirty dishes in the kitchen sink and on all the kitchen counters. The roaches got in the cereal boxes and the safest bet for any kind of edible meal might be a pack of Twinkies or a newly opened can of Hormel chili. I did have my own space, though, even though it was not really hospitable. I slept in the attic on a mattress with springs poking out of it. I'd memorized where they were and would contort my body to avoid getting stuck in the middle of the night. Rats and mice lived in my closet. And after a while, I hardly noticed them.

Night after night, I'd lie in the dark and think about how I could escape from this life. Not by committing suicide, but by running away before it got too late. I became so obsessed with escaping that I shared my feelings with Mrs. Gossart, my school principal. There was probably no hope of my doing anything but just living with my situation, but at least I knew I had someone whom I trusted to share my deepest feelings with.

My grandparents had devised a plan to rescue me. . .a "runaway plan." I'd been talking with Mrs. Gossart for many weeks and trusted her, so I thought I'd mention the plan to her. I remember thinking "Oh geez, she's going to think I'm crazy," but I wanted her approval. For the first time in a long time, I was excited about my future.

She listened in the way that a loving aunt would. There was no judgment, no scolding, and no denigrating words that put me in my thirteen-year-old place. I knew I could trust her. But then she stunned me with a surprising reaction.

Mrs. Gossart took my hands in hers and I felt protected. There was a small part of me that wanted to remember a time I felt that with my mother, but I couldn't, for the life of me, remember anything that sincerely loving. The only time my mother showed any kind of physical affection or attachment or connection was when she was lashing out in anger or reaching out for forgiveness.

"Bridgette, you must stick to your guns, no matter what! Go for it!" she said.

I looked at her and blinked, as a cat does when it's uncertain whether it wants to leap onto your lap or scratch your face.

The plan was for my grandparents to get custody of me. I just prayed that we would win the case. I told Mrs. Gossart that my granddad was an attorney and that he would represent me. He knew I had to obtain an emergency hearing, and that in order for me to take my mother to court, I had to become a missing child. I trusted him implicitly. She agreed, as she knew my granddad well and had much respect for him.

So, I would be, in effect, divorcing my own mother. I would become emancipated.

I would be free.

The only problem was that most states only allow emancipations for those who are a little older. I was only thirteen, but I just couldn't take my living conditions anymore. I couldn't continue to watch my mother suffer from her own hand and from the blows of others. I couldn't watch her kill herself.

So, one night...it wasn't the first...I found her passed out. And I ran away. With Mrs. Gossart's words echoing in my head, my plan was to stay away from my mother's home until I could obtain a court date to have custody...my custody...removed from her and transferred, well, to almost anyone else.

Then I began house hopping in earnest. Sometimes I'd stay with my grandparents, and sometimes with my close circle of friends and their families. The houses I lived in now were the white picket fence houses that my friends lived in. Their families generously and lovingly welcomed me into their lives and their parents helped to conceal me from my mother and from the authorities. It was just a continuation of what I already had experience with. Since my mom was a less than stellar parent, we had a few previous encounters with child protective services where her custody was in question and hanging by a thread.

My first night away from home—in the summer before eighth grade—was surreal. After school, I went to my friend Karyn's house and snacked on some Cheetos and Pepsi while we watched TV and waited for her parents to come home. I was so anxious, so nervous, but at the same time excited.

Karyn was a few years older than me and very popular and pretty. I knew her from the ice skating rink. She lived in a very nice, big house in an upscale neighborhood. Her parents were very professional and worldly. They didn't ask a lot of questions and I didn't volunteer any information. Karyn's older brother was really cute and all the girls swooned over him. We hung out in her room as if it were any other ordinary night, and talked about boys, fashion, and makeup. Karyn had a huge family and siblings were coming and going all the time. Thankfully no one paid much attention to my presence, which was a huge relief.

As the family sat down for dinner, I took in the picture. Hot food was in bowls and platters and everyone was passing around rolls and potatoes and other side dishes. The sounds and conversation became muffled and my ears started to ring. I could see everyone around me eating and laughing, but I felt very separate from all the activity. It's as if I was a spectator and not a participant.

"Bridgette, are you OK?" Karyn asked.

I was only slightly aware of everyone looking at me as the ringing in my ears increased.

"Bridge?" Karyn shook my shoulder.

The ringing stopped. Suddenly everything became loud again: the conversations, the laughter, the silverware clinking and ice cubes rattling in glass tumblers. I looked at everyone amidst the commotion. And then I smiled.

I was taking control of my life.

In total, I was on the "run" for about six weeks, and each family I stayed with immediately treated me as one of their own. And at every moment that each door to each family opened, it also opened a gigantic risk to them because of me. These friends and their families not only became crucial to my survival, but to theirs. If they were found harboring a missing child, the consequences would be life changing. In spite of that, it was true proof of parents willing to risk everything, even their own lives, to save their children. And even children they never bore.

Sometimes I'd even take a day off from staying in my friends' houses. I'd grab my backpack and go to the beach. I would take the bus from New Carrollton or Baltimore and head to Ocean City. I'd use my backpack as a pillow. There were even moments when I imagined what I'd feel like if this bus would take me at that very moment to Los Angeles or Denver or New York. Hearing and seeing the waves crash against the shore reminded me that there was a whole world out there, an entire planet to be a part of, and that my problems, big or small, were really inconsequential in the big scheme of things. I loved to walk in the sand and feel it give way with each slow step. Some days it was cold and stiff, as if I were walking on concrete after a summer rain. Other times, my feet would sink into it and I felt as if Mother Earth was hugging me. There were times when I zoned out just sitting near a sand dune and listening to the waves and seagulls in search of bags of discarded food. The smell of the ocean cleared my head and helped to center me, especially when I started to fret.

Sometimes, in these weak moments, a little voice in my head said, "Just go home. This is too much trouble. You probably won't win anyway." But then I remembered my granddad and all the people who loved me who weren't even related by blood.

I officially became a missing child when the cops couldn't find me after repeated tries. I don't know if my mother really knew where I was or if she was just too embroiled in her own problems. All I had to do was stay on the run until my court date, about two months after I ran away.

Whenever I slept at my grandparents' house, I kept the upstairs door ajar in case I had to make a quick escape. My bedroom was upstairs in the attic, and the tattered, old mattress that served as my bed was pressed against the edge of the doorjamb. I slept with my head next to it so I could hear the cops or my mother if they showed up unexpectedly. The local police force would send officers to the house after I went "missing" and my grandmother would meet them at the door with scorn and distrust.

"I don't know why you think we would harbor a missing child," she snorted at the beleaguered officers. "My husband is a respected attorney. Why in high heaven would you even think he would involve himself and risk his practice and his reputation? And if you're as competent as you should be as public servants, you might have found my dear granddaughter by now."

Then she would shake her head in disgust as she invited the cops in for a look-see, which they did with half-hearted efforts before doffing their hats with apologetic murmurs and hightailed it out the door. During these surprise visits, I'd run out the back door and hide under the neighbor's overgrown pine trees. But it wasn't until around the tenth visit that I actually got close enough to hear the mocking, sarcastic tone that my grandmother had in her voice as she chided the officers for their failed attempts at finding me. She should have won an Oscar. After she chided them and ushered them out of the house, she'd call for me and giggle, as if the situation was some sort of game.

The night before the hearing, my grandmother acted as if everything was "normal." No one really discussed their feelings or fears; in fact, they didn't ever really express much emotion at all.

And finally, the day came. Granddad represented me. He prepared me for what could happen by explaining both sides of the case and warned me that the day was going to be the hardest day of my life, but that it wouldn't be the only one.

My granddad said, "Be strong, Bridgette, just like you always are." That's it. My family wasn't big on emotions because they felt that emotions made a person "weak." I know Granddad loved my mother very much and never wanted to hurt her. In fact, I'm sure that was one of the hardest days of his life. . . taking his own daughter to court on behalf of her child. I don't want to underestimate that. He was no more on my side than he was on hers. I believe he loved us equally, but his goal was to help me out of a situation that I could not navigate on my own since I was only thirteen. Granddad wanted to give me every opportunity in life to break the vicious cycle that my mother and aunts had created and lived in. He never intended to hurt anyone. He wouldn't hurt a fly. But today, I couldn't sugarcoat anything. My mother was sick and broken in so many ways and I felt as if I was crucifying her with my upcoming testimony, but if I didn't break away, I was afraid I'd become her in ten years—or less.

And Granddad was right. The court date arrived. I walked into the courtroom, and came face-to-face with my mom, who tried her best to pretty herself up for the hearing. The minute I saw her, my heart crumbled into a million pieces. This woman standing before me was a vibrant, beautiful, kind, funny woman. She had so much potential, so much talent, so much to offer this world. There was so much love in her heart that it broke me to look into her eyes. I knew that this moment would crush her forever. I knew that we would forever be emotionally separated by a wedge bigger than the Atlantic Ocean. No matter what happened, this moment would be life changing for both of us.

The weight of what I was about to do came at me like a roaring freight train. I swore to the judge to tell the truth, the whole truth, and nothing but the truth. And then, with my ears ringing and tears stinging my eyes, I took the stand.

Against my own mother.

I remembered what Granddad told me. I told the truth. And as I did, I looked my mom in the eyes. Everything came pouring out, and I couldn't stop myself. I'd held it in for too long. I told the judge about our constant apartment and house hopping, about her substance abuse, about her abusive boyfriends, and how I always felt unsafe in my own home. Spilling out of my mouth came recounts of our living situation—the constant anxiety, the drinking, and the beatings. Even though the judge had to remain impartial and objective, the few times I managed to look at him, I noticed there was darkness in his face. Pain. Understanding. Shock. Disgrace and disillusionment that what was happening to me ever had to happen. There was a part of me that wanted to bolt out of that courtroom because I felt as if I was betraying my mom irreparably and wounding her forever.

When I caught her gaze, I could see the pain in her eyes and a new expression. It was the face of someone whose light had just been switched off, whose heart had been stabbed one too many times because the reality was too raw, too painful. This was a hurt that cut right to her soul and changed her forever.

Because hers was a heart that knew it was all true.

After I testified, the judge turned toward me and asked, "Bridgette, should you be taken away from your mother permanently?" And I replied, "Yes."

It was the worst day of my life.

And it was also the last time I'd hear from my mother for a very long time.

My grandparents were awarded custody. Granddad did everything he could to prepare me for life, especially so since his initial cancer diagnosis a few years before. Many days and nights he would take me to the ice rink for my figure skating lessons, and he would sit on the bench with his legs crossed, book in hand, and cough his lungs out. He coughed up so much phlegm from the cancer and became so weak, but there was always a smile on his face. He never, ever complained. He took me to church on Sundays, helped me with my homework every night, and taught me to always stay curious and question everything.

When we'd work on my homework, he would never give me the answer or even tell me if my answer was correct. He would say, "You tell me if it's correct!" And then he would ask me why I believed the answer was right or wrong. If I didn't know he would immediately take me to Prince George's County Library and have me look it up for myself. To this day, I love books and I love to read. Sitting in a bookstore or library for hours on end while perusing tons of books has always brought me peace and comfort. I could spend days there and then go back for more. There were no shortcuts to education. I loved his method. I loved that he taught me to fend for myself. He would always say, "The only person in the world that you can ever really rely on is yourself."

My grandfather was full of life. He was six feet four with a lean, slender build. He had thinning gray hair and often wore a hat when it was chilly outside. His wardrobe was very simple but always appropriate. I don't think he owned more than one pair of shoes. Along with his ever-present glasses, he looked like a dignified university professor. He was always smiling and in a good mood. He relished in the little things. . .enjoyed every moment. He didn't need much. In fact, he hardly needed anything at all. He would hand over his entire paycheck to my grandmother each payday and only keep $10 for himself to last a week or so. He was perfectly fine living off of peanut butter and jelly sandwiches and a tall glass of milk. He loved to play board games. We used to play them for hours and hours. Monopoly, checkers, Chutes and Ladders. We would also do puzzle books together. I don't think I ever saw him in a bad mood. Negativity was not in his personality. He was incredibly kind to others and would give a homeless person his last penny.

Granddad would teach me success strategies. "Bridgette," he'd say, "you're a Do-be. Not a Don't-be. Don't pay attention to what anyone else is doing. You do the right thing no matter what. Your life is up to you. Choose your path wisely. I know you will. Because you're a Do-be." I think he must have been referring to a Dr. Seuss term because he read those books to me constantly, especially *Oh, the Places You'll Go!*

He worked to instill in me compassion, drive, perseverance, and dedication. And he also showed me the power of true love and forgiveness. Despite my mother's state of existence, despite her mistakes, her drug and alcohol abuse, and her treatment of me, he really, truly loved her. I never heard a word of criticism from him toward her, and she certainly was no angel.

Granddad was always my emotional support. He was the parent figure that my mom and dad should have been. After long days at work, he'd return home to take me to all my figure skating lessons and basketball games. I never missed having a traditional doting parent as the other skaters did, because I had my very own doting granddad.

He was diagnosed with Stage IV cancer that started in his colon and quickly metastasized to his brain before treatment. Despite Granddad's sickness, he was fully committed to taking this last act of support and love for me. In fact, much of the strategy around my "missing" status was to push the court hearing to an earlier date before my grandfather passed away. Over the next few weeks, Granddad became frailer. He spent more time in bed and became so very weak. But he still had a glimmer in his eye and lit up when he saw me. I couldn't imagine life without him and spent as much time as I could with him. And as he took his last breath, I held his hand and forced myself to remember this moment, to remember his love for me, to remember holding his hand as he crossed the veil into the ether. And I was holding his hand as he took his last breath with my grandmother and the priest by his side. He was buried at Arlington National Cemetery with a 21-gun salute for honorably serving in the United States Navy.

And in the span of just a few months, I experienced the second worst day of my young life.

BRIDGETTE PEARCE

CHAPTER 8

Go Your Own Way

It's funny how meaningful events in your life can be affected by your parents, no matter how old you—or they—are. I've known people who hated their parents and loved their in-laws and vice versa. I've known people who shunned their parents, only to be "adopted" by strangers who proved to be the best parents in the world. What I do know about parents and the relationships they have with their kids is this: it can be complicated.

What any of us ends up with is a gamble. I've learned so much in my life to last ten lifetimes, and I always try to be as balanced a parent as I can be. Living through challenges and hardship made a huge impact on my life, and it helped me realize what traits I wanted to develop so I could be the best person, wife, mom, friend, and relative to everyone in my life.

I learned many life lessons from my mothers.

That's right. Both of them.

Kent, my husband, was a stand-up guy from the moment I met him. Still is. He had character, values, and an ethical "code" that not a lot of people possess. I figured that parents who raised a man of his caliber must be top notch themselves and couldn't wait to meet them when he and I got serious.

Fast-forward to when our oldest son, Tye, was just under two years old. He was born with a hole in his heart, a condition called a "ventricular septal defect," or VSD. The hole was in the wall that separates the two lower chambers of the heart. In normal development, the inter-chamber wall closes before the baby is born and acts as a shield so that oxygen-rich blood doesn't mix with oxygen-poor blood. If the hole doesn't close, it can cause pressure within the heart and reduced oxygen in the body. Tye's pediatrician thought it would close as he grew older, but instead it increased in size. By the time he was eighteen months old, the doctor said he needed open heart surgery because the condition could escalate to the point where it could kill our baby.

Honest to God, whenever you hear the old adage that no parent wants their children to suffer and they wish they could take the pain away, nothing could be truer. Kent and I were fraught with anxiety and worry, and yet neither of us wanted to let our little guy see us like this. We wanted him to know we loved him, and although he couldn't talk in sentences yet, we knew he fed off what we were feeling and the expressions on our faces.

My mom did not show up at the hospital on surgery day. Given her situation, I can understand why. We'd found the best pediatric heart surgeon at Johns Hopkins Hospital and had to trust that we'd done all we could to get Tye through this ordeal with a good outcome. I couldn't even bring myself to think of the alternative.

Kent's parents came to the hospital to be with us for moral support after the surgery. While we sat in the waiting room hour after hour, Kent left to get a bagel. We were so exhausted but didn't dare fall asleep. The clock ticked as loudly as a door slamming and it made me even more nervous. Every time doctors came through the waiting room doors, we looked up expectantly but each time were let down when we saw them approach the other families awaiting updates.

After a few more hours with no news, we all started to silently panic. Kent and I checked in with the nurses' station every hour, but all they told him was that the family would have to continue waiting to hear the official word from the surgeon. I was so thankful for my in-laws, and of course for Kent. While I forced myself to believe that it was probably for the best that my mom wasn't there, my heart also ached because of it. My ears started ringing and the anxiety of old started to creep in.

And at that moment, the pediatric surgeon stepped from behind the OR doors with a weary smile on his face. Tye is now eighteen years old and stands a strapping six feet three.

To this day, I grapple with how often and for how long I should invite my mom to be part of my family's life. It was the year of a milestone birthday for me, and Kent planned a big party in our backyard. It took place in the evening and we hosted all our adult friends and no kids—but our own, of course. The atmosphere was relaxed and our guests caught up with us and each other as they sipped cocktails in the warmth of the early evening. We couldn't have asked for a better day. The live band occupied the corner of our yard beneath some ancient trees and played cover music: U2, Nickelback, and Fleetwood Mac. We relinquished all the cooking to a caterer so we could lounge the evening away and enjoy pulled pork sliders and crunchy coleslaw with maple baked beans. Dessert was home-style apple crisp and warm, homemade chocolate chip cookies. Birthday cake was vanilla with fresh, macerated strawberries and had sweet buttercream icing. But truth be told, on that day, I would have asked for one little thing. If it was a perfect world.

My mom, Jeannie.

A few of my cousins turned out for the big day, but my mother did not. And I have to admit—I'm embarrassed to admit really—that I didn't invite her. Because the world is far from perfect, and I just couldn't rely on *her* reliability either punctuality-wise or behavior-wise, to risk a big event on such an unknown variable.

I didn't know if she'd react with understated sentimentality because the day reminded her of the grandchildren that she rarely saw, or that the "haves" would act as a constant reminder that she was one of the "have-nots." After she would start drinking, there was no telling what would come out of her mouth. Unpredictable.

She and I kept in touch over the years through Facebook. Sometimes she'd even end up in the homes of people that she would ingratiate herself with or exchange "favors" with to gain a roof over her head for a few days.

And over the years, I was used to her responding to some pictures of the kids' basketball games, dance recitals, or my pictures with my closest girlfriends. Her responses were never lengthy, but the fact that they existed helped me cope with the emotional stress of knowing that my mother was a homeless woman in Washington, D.C.

I didn't know why she didn't respond to the party pictures I posted on Facebook. I wasn't trying to brag, I was just trying to share an important event in my life with those friends and family who knew and loved me and couldn't make it to the party. I don't know if she felt guilty, incapable of being near me, incapable of showing emotion, or if she just outright didn't care. It was also possible that she didn't have it within her to care anymore, and that made me so very sad.

Our relationship over the years was rocky at best, and since that day at thirteen when I garnered my freedom from her, we rarely saw each other. We kept in touch from time to time and I knew that she was as OK as anyone else in her situation could be. Mom never once showed up at my doorstep to demand help. She made her own way on the streets and I've never wanted to assume that she would want her life any other way. The subject of any kind of assistance never came up between us, so all I could do was assume that she was living the life that she knew how to live and to do anything else would not be true to who she was.

Still, I always felt there was an air of optimism about her and that she never gave up. The situations she found herself living in and around would probably have killed the average person by now, but my mom is a scrapper and very independent. It's very possible that after all of the abuse and the beatings and the near-death encounters with former boyfriends that living on the street was its own form of freedom for her.

But I have to point out that in the worst years of my childhood with my mom it was like living with Dr. Jekyll and Mr. Hyde. Although she had an addiction to alcohol and drugs, she was functional during the day. We'd go shopping and sometimes we'd stop at McDonald's for a couple of Happy Meals. Our relationship during daylight hours was kind of normal! But the night brought on the dysfunction. With darkness came the uncertainty, the abuse, the violence, and the general upset. I never knew if she would awaken in the morning when the sun rose.

About a year after the court decision for my grandparents to take custody of me, my beloved granddad died. Since I was no longer physically in her life, my mom pretty much became homeless. She would bounce from boyfriend's house to boyfriend's house, and sometimes she lived on the street, a precursor to what she's done for the last three decades. When she would break up with a boyfriend, he'd kick her out and she'd go to a shelter where she'd live as long as they would let her.

Mom was a very talented hairdresser, but her life was a result of the choices she made, both good and bad. She did her best to give me an ideal childhood, but it just didn't work. I don't hate my mom, I do love her very much. I know she tried. My granddad, although he was not an emotional, showy type, loved my mother with all his heart to the day he died.

Every Christmas, she'd make hot chocolate with the little marshmallows on top. We'd drink it by the TV set as *Rudolph the Red-Nosed Reindeer* played, which every kid knew meant it was the start of the Christmas season. One day after school, Mom and I decided to escape the ever-cold weather outside and pretend to do some Christmas shopping.

As we walked through the doors of the mall, we laid eyes on a fairy-tale scene, with twinkling Christmas lights and the smell of fresh pine (which probably wasn't fresh but at least it was from pine-scented Glade candles and it worked!). Mom looked like a kid in a candy store as she walked past all of the Christmas tree displays and decorations and mannequins of

Santa Claus and his reindeer in the store windows. I looked at her face and her eyes twinkled as if she'd been given the keys to the kingdom.

"See honey?" she said. "One day we'll have a giant Christmas tree in our living room that reaches the ceiling, and you and I can decorate it with whatever you want...colored lights... look at these little twinkling lights! And tinsel! And whatever decorations you want! We could even put popcorn on a string if you promise not to eat all of it!"

Part of me was hopeful that this scenario she was painting in her head would come true... that the abuse would stop, that the pain would stop, that the drugs and alcohol would stop... and that we could live a normal family life. Just Mom and me. But even though I was still only a kid, I knew that it probably would never be and so I went along with her pretty pictures of what she hoped. I told her of my dreams that it would be nice to have a bike and maybe some makeup...and I asked her what *she* wanted for Christmas.

Mom stopped and turned to me and a smile that graced her face for the last few minutes faded a little bit, but her eyes twinkled even more.

"Oh sweetie," she said. "You don't need to get me *anything*. You are my gift every Christmas and I love you so much! You're all I need."

We walked a little further, hand in hand, until we passed by a candy store. Inside there were mechanized elves, Mr. and Mrs. Claus, and some reindeer along with colored lights surrounding the glass containers of divinity, peppermint sticks, candy canes, chocolates, caramel, and every other sweet treat that would send any kid into a sugar coma. Mom said excitedly, "Come on honey, let's get something sweet!"

We bought some chocolate-covered caramels and peanut clusters. I felt like Charlie Bucket from *Willy Wonka and the Chocolate Factory* when he found a dollar in the gutter and ran to the candy store to buy his very own chocolate bar. We walked over to the nearest bench and plopped down on it to watch the holiday shoppers and savor our sweets. I took a tiny bite of the first peanut cluster, just enough to break off a single peanut. I let the milk chocolate soften and melt onto my tongue, never chewing any of it. When it had all melted, I started nibbling the peanut in tiny bites, so the experience would last longer.

I looked over at my mother and realized she'd finished half her stash. She had a dreamy look in her eyes and I realized she'd been watching me and not the hundreds of shoppers walking past. She reached over and brushed my hair out of my eyes.

"I love you sweetheart," she said softly.

Mom was not of the stock to show emotion, and neither was Granddad. But it didn't mean they didn't have a deep capacity for love. So, this unexpected moment of tenderness, mixed with the heady rush of the crowds, twinkling lights, Christmas music, and relative normalcy of the interaction made my senses swirl. But before I got too comfortable, Mom grabbed my hand and jumped to her feet.

"I have something to show you!" she said, as she yanked me off the bench.

We strolled past the candle shop and a Foot Locker, then a pricy jewelry store before stopping at a clothing boutique.

"Remember what I promised you?" Mom asked.

I had no idea what she was talking about. There were so many promises, so many disappointments, that after a while, I stopped believing. And I stopped listening.

Mom led me to a rack of leather bomber jackets and pulled a weathered brown one to hold up to me. The jacket was almost identical to the one that Tom Cruise wore in *Top Gun*. It was the must-have of the season, and all the fashion magazines showed glossy paparazzi photos of glamorous movie stars wearing them, even with beaded evening gowns at award shows or at a fancy red carpet movie premiere.

I was in heaven. My mom told me to try a few on and pick my favorite one. I couldn't believe it. I was so excited and felt as if we'd won the lottery. I tried on a handful of styles in the dressing room as Nat King Cole crooned "Chestnuts Roasting on an Open Fire" on the speakers above my head. But the music and cramped dressing room didn't make one bit of difference in my mood—in my mind, I was on a runway in Paris and nothing could ever go wrong again.

Mom was in the dressing room next to mine and picked her favorite style: a dark green fitted bomber jacket with distressed brass snaps and thick knitted cuffs. She knocked on my door and when I opened it, she struck a supermodel pose before twirling around to show off her new look. She was always hip and had a beautiful figure, face, and perfectly highlighted hair.

I wasn't quite sure how she intended to pay for this jacket and I was afraid to even ask. As we brought our jackets to the cashier, mom handed the clerk a credit card. I was completely baffled. I had no idea my mother owned a credit card. *Where did she get it?* I wondered, and actually found myself getting a little dizzy because I'd been holding my breath in anticipation.

We stood motionless as the clerk swiped the card through the reader. It beeped. She wiped the card against her shirt and swiped it again. Another beep. Then she tried typing the card number into the reader by hand. It beeped a third time. Mom took it back from the clerk and muttered something about bank delays. As she opened her pocketbook to stuff the card away, I noticed the name imprinted on its front belonged to a man I'd never heard of.

Ah. So that's it, then, I thought. Maybe Mom had a new boyfriend. . .or at least some guy was trying to be her boyfriend and showing off.

The three beeps and my mom's look of. . .what? Disgust? Anger? Shame? All these wiped out the joy of our Christmas jaunt at the mall. *I didn't want that stupid jacket anyway,* I tried to convince myself. *I don't want to look like everyone else.* We didn't utter a word to each other as we made our way through the mall to go home. As we passed a trash can, I let the bag of candy slip from my fingers into the hollow, and I wondered if my mom would ever truly get her life together.

I never knew what substances Mom tortured herself with, but I knew it wasn't just wine and cigarettes. One day, I asked her boyfriend what drugs she was on and he said "everything." Pot? "Everything," he repeated. Heroin? "Everything." Cocaine? "Everything." I don't know if he was just trying to get rid of me or shock me or disgust me, but a small part of me thought that even he was too embarrassed to admit that he and Mom were drug addicts and that their actions put me in danger. This was the very same boyfriend that put all of her belongings in the front yard and lit them on fire with as much nonchalance as if he just made himself a sandwich.

When Granddad died, I basically stopped hearing from my mother. I didn't hear from her after that for many, many years. We had no relationship; she never reached out. She was humiliated, I think, and proud, even though she struggled with self-esteem issues and all the other issues that abused women suffer from.

I never know exactly where she is these days, but I do know her regular spots. I've invited her for brunch or lunch with me and the kids, and when she decides to accompany us, she dresses and acts as if nothing is wrong at all. She behaves as if she's a regular suburban grandma with beautiful grandkids and a lovely home. I think she's been abusing alcohol and drugs for so long that this scenario is one she actually *believes* is true. She doesn't want to admit to herself that her life is what it is as a homeless, female senior citizen.

My children used to ask about their grandma a lot. They'd visit their friends and meet their grandparents. Some lived with the families, others had their own homes and could still live independently. And our kids would always be curious.

"Mommy," my daughter started one Saturday morning as I made cheese omelets for breakfast. *Dora the Explorer* was playing on the big TV in the living room.

"Yes, sweetheart?" I replied.

"Mommy, why doesn't Gigi live with us?"

Mom liked the name "Gigi" instead of grandma, gama, gammy, nana, or mom-mom. Those terms of endearment weren't endearing in her mind. They made her feel old, and life was hard enough as it was.

"Um. . .well, um. Honey, do you want bacon with your omelet?" I felt tears stinging my eyes.

Then my son Kolt chimed in. "I love Gigi. Why can't she come stay here?"

They were so young. They didn't understand.

"Mommy?" they said in unison.

This was it. I had to pull myself together. I couldn't let it all crumble now. Not after all I'd been through.

"Baby," I started, "Baby, Gigi likes where she's living now. She has friends there. She wouldn't want you to leave your friends, right?"

This was uncharted territory. In all aspects of my life, I had it together. My tendency toward OCD made me very organized, very orderly. There were plans and backup plans for every aspect of my life and of my family's lives.

Getting this question out of the blue completely threw me off course.

"Plus," I continued, "Gigi loves her animals and she lives in a place now where she can help rescue them. She is very important in her community. You can't just ask her to leave all that behind."

I hated having to stretch the truth with my children, but they were too young to understand the harsh realities of their grandma's existence.

They looked pensive for a few moments until I served breakfast. And that pensiveness instantly changed as they grabbed their forks and started gobbling down their breakfasts as if nothing happened.

Thank God it would be a few more years until they discovered the truth.

BRIDGETTE PEARCE

CHAPTER 9

The Aftermath

In spite of the fact that my court date and its aftermath were incredibly stressful, one of my takeaways was that I was no longer afraid of making big moves anymore. It didn't matter how risky these moves seemed, I knew that because I survived the "divorce" ordeal without having a lightning bolt strike me dead, I probably could survive a lot worse.

At a time when most girls my age focused on what new trendy outfits they wanted for school or what shades of lipstick they would buy after they were given permission to wear makeup, it was time for this thirteen-year-old to plan for her future.

I had one more year left at St. Mark's and then it was time to make another big decision: Where would I attend high school? Because of Granddad's deteriorating health, I knew I had to stay close to him to help out with his care. This included taking him to doctors' appointments, helping with his medication, helping him get dressed, preparing meals for him, and just being there for him whenever I could. I would do anything for him.

But I also knew that I could not attend Northwestern High School, which was the school zone where we lived. The area was depressed and fraught with dilapidated neighborhoods, rampant homelessness, gangs, and crime. It was once the epitome of happy, 1950s America, with healthy, middle-class families living their lives of jobs at the factories, homemade lunches of baloney sandwiches and potato chips, and *Leave It to Beaver*, but in recent decades, the economy failed and the middle class moved elsewhere. What was left were old-timers who couldn't afford to move from finances or age, as well as new residents from urban areas who took advantage of housing and living prices. Many students who attended Northwestern (including my mother and some of her sisters) never graduated. Some got pregnant and dropped out, others got married and dropped out, still others disappeared from the neighborhood altogether, never to be seen again.

I took it upon myself to enroll in High Point High School, which was one town away... about twenty minutes by car. The only way I could get approval to attend a different high school (out of our zone) was to take Russian. That was fine by me! I would do anything to graduate early, even if it meant taking a language I would never use (probably). But truth be told, I did manage, decades later, to understand some of the Russian dialogue in *Orange Is the New Black*, so it wasn't a total loss!

Every day, I illegally drove myself to school. It was a huge risk. The security and administrative staff at High Point High School turned a blind eye when they saw me drive to and from school, but I didn't have that same protection at Northwestern. Sure, kids were bused to and from school, but because I lived in a different school zone altogether, there were no buses that even got near my house. My grandmother couldn't drive me back and forth because she was taking care of Granddad. I had no other choice than to risk tickets and possibly even suspension from school. Thank God neither of these possibilities ever transpired, because I was just trying to survive and it was hard enough with the daily challenges of school, transportation, and being my Granddad's caregiver. Part of this lesson also involved looking beyond the established paths to success. As I finished ninth grade at High Point, I realized that public school was not for me. I attended St. Mark's, the little Catholic school, since I was a child. Its small classes, its passionate teachers, and close-knit friends I had were just some of the happy surroundings and interactions I lived and learned in every single day. I absolutely loved to read; *The Year of Janie's Diary* was an early favorite, and I also loved *Flowers in the Attic* by V.C. Andrews. When I read books, the stories carried me away to new adventures far, far away from my real life, and I imagined myself as the heroine in them. I saw myself facing the same challenges as the young girls in these books and acted out in my mind what I would do in their shoes. I wasn't wishing my life was exactly like theirs, because I was too realistic by nature to know that we can't change what's past. But the chance to dream about what my life could be like was a place I wanted to occupy as much as I could so that I could make the plans needed to make that new life a reality.

And the discipline! I loved how strict it was. Most kids would have hated it, but not me. St. Mark's was a no-nonsense, stick-to-the-rules, stay-in-a-single-file environment that raised phenomenal students. Detention was punishment if you misbehaved, skipped class, or talked back to the teachers, and all the students knew that there was zero tolerance for anyone who misbehaved, even in a small way. I remember a boy in my class turned his head slightly to look out the window. Without him noticing, the teacher, a nun, slowly walked over to his desk with a wooden ruler in her hand and spoke in a loud, stern voice, "What exactly are you looking at, mister?

The lesson on the chalkboard is not outside!" She smacked the ruler onto his desk with such a loud thump that it made my classmate jump in his seat. He never turned his head during class again. The nuns were *not* to be messed with.

You'd better have your eyes focused on the teacher with your head up and your back straight. God was always the foundation and students learned to respect their teachers, their peers, and, most importantly, themselves. Part of the impact that discipline had on me was not only behavioral and societal, but it impacted my learning in a major way. Not only did I love to read because novels and mysteries took me to all the corners of the Earth and expanded my imagination, I loved reading because there were so many interesting things to learn. Call me a geek or a book nerd, whatever you want. One of my absolute favorite pastimes in school involved not only reading books, but also reading encyclopedias! They fascinated me just as much then as they do now. Today's encyclopedias, including Google and YouTube, would take up all my spare time if I let it!

High Point was nothing like St. Mark's. It was vast, and discipline could not be easily enforced. For example, there was a lobby around the side of the school that we referred to as "the burnout lobby." The kids that hung out there were into smoking cigarettes, pot, and drinking. I wouldn't be caught dead in that lobby! Many kids at High Point dealt drugs. There were also lots of fights and stabbings at parties. There was no order at the school and it was almost as if the inmates took over the prison. I think that most teachers felt hopeless and were happy to escape at the end of each day with their lives intact.

In what I found was somewhat typical of public schools in Prince George's County, many students strayed. You'd see kids sneak off campus for lunch or other questionable activities. Truancy was rampant and the teachers were overloaded with students and demanding teaching milestones they had to enforce in order to receive annual funding for their classes. There simply were too many students to corral, discipline, and teach. Because I was used to a very strict academic environment, I knew I couldn't stay there long. The thought of even being here for four years was one I didn't want to consider. Time was of the essence and I had a path to pave, so in tenth grade, I devised a plan to "test out" and leave high school early. I had to move on with my life.

I was compelled to achieve success in my own life, and no one could do it for me. After lots of research, I was ready to execute my plan. I successfully passed the GED in tenth grade with flying colors. I had zero tolerance for naysayers. I didn't want people's opinions and I certainly didn't need the judgment that I knew was constantly bubbling beneath their expressions and feigned interest.

"Oh Bridgette, why don't you go to cosmetology school like your mom?" or "You know the GED won't get you anywhere. You need to really graduate from high school before any university will accept you," or "Why, you're only sixteen! You barely have your driver's license," or "Why are you rushing? Enjoy your childhood a little," or, from strangers, "Oh sweetheart, what could you possibly know at this age about college...or even real life?"

One of the reasons I worked so hard was because I knew it was human nature for people to think this way about me (and my mom) and I wanted to prove all of them wrong. It wasn't an ego thing. It wasn't an attempt to be "better" than my mother or rub my success in her face. I knew that, in her sober moments, she wanted nothing but the best for me, and I wanted to make her and my granddad proud of me. I also I knew I would never turn out like her. There was no way on God's green earth that I would ever let that happen. But I am so very grateful that she did make me the woman I am today. It really is because of the struggles and hardship that I gained strength, focus, and clarity. I was always in control of myself, and always prepared to do what I had to do to break the cycle.

My scores on the GED were extremely high, and shortly after I passed, I started receiving scholarship offers. One of the colleges I applied to was the University of Maryland. It was a prestigious campus and only five minutes from home. UMCP had one of the best mechanical engineering programs around. I had no idea how long it would take to process my application, much less how long it would take for admissions' counselors to respond with a "yes" or a "no." The wait was killing me, so I decided to get busy for the summer. I started taking classes at the local community college. After only a month, I received my acceptance letter from the University of Maryland. The University of Maryland was the only university I applied to. I knew my scores were high enough to be accepted. So, I took a chance.

The university offered me a spot in its summer mechanical engineering program for women and they were also willing to pay me to attend! Since the university was trying to recruit more women into the field of engineering, part of the program involved my getting paid to attend school. I accepted and transferred my credits immediately. In the fall, I received grants for college, so most of my tuition (including books) was paid for. The remainder I paid for myself with money I'd saved as well as a few small student loans.

DETACHED

The very first day that I set foot on that campus and walked to my first class, I knew I had arrived. I felt so excited...so SMART! Here I was—among scholars—and I was a part of it. ME! I excelled and flourished. The discipline I learned at St. Mark's proved an amazing foundation for higher learning, especially since I was still so young. I never even finished tenth grade, and here I was, a freshman at the University of Maryland.

Wow.

The happiness and pride I felt that first day on campus was overwhelming. My schedule was full and I had a strict daily routine. I would always stop at the little bagel place on my way to class and get a poppy seed bagel for breakfast. I would sit in that big lecture hall with my books, my pens and pencils, and my bagel. At the time, it's what made me complete. I was happy.

But during that first year after Granddad died, a weird thing happened. My grandmother had always been a grumpy, surly woman. She was always critical of everyone, my granddad included. She was fairly tall with thick, gray hair and average looks. She didn't wear much makeup besides a little rouge, nor did she take much pride in herself or her appearance. Grandma had diabetes and arthritis in her hands and wore muumuu dresses most of the time. She was fairly lazy, and loved her soap operas. Her health was surely compromised by the fact that she ate a lot of sweets and never exercised or even took walks. Every room in the house was complete filth, but she didn't seem to mind. This was how she was used to living. It didn't matter if the bathtub had a dark, dirty ring around it or if the dishes in the sink had the same food stuck to them for months.

Once Granddad was gone, she became much angrier. She was mad at me, mad at the world, mad at everything. It's as if, with his passing, she no longer had anyone to pick on, to abuse, to control. Many times when loved ones die, their passings change their family and friends. I've seen friends who were normally angry at the world or unappreciative of their families/jobs/opportunities do a complete turnaround and soften—at least a little. They're more contemplative. More appreciative of the people around them and of the realization that every moment we live is a gift and certainly that tomorrow is never promised.

I don't know why I expected her to react any differently to his passing. I guess I was hoping that such a loss would work to make her more appreciative about her family and her life. But I was wrong. Where she'd turn her anger toward Granddad in his life, she now focused it with laser-point aim at me. It felt as if she wanted to destroy everything he loved.

And her way of destroying me didn't involve traditional mistreatment or abuse. Sure, she'd always treated me with a certain amount of disdain and irritation, so if anything, I expected her to ignore me now that Granddad wasn't around for her to pick on. But strangely enough, she became obsessed with me. She wanted me to be a swimsuit model. She wanted me to be perfect. She wanted me to be a "STAR." In a very short time, she morphed from "Mommie Dearest" to "Mama Rose." It was far worse than anything I'd experienced with my own mother, who, at worst, was verbally abusive when she was under the influence, but otherwise always very loving and kind when she was sober.

If my grandmother saw me head out the door to school wearing a sweatshirt and jeans or a comfy boyfriend button-down shirt and leggings, she would scream at me and demand that I come back inside and change. She wanted me to wear tight shirts and skintight jeans 24/7. She always wanted to see me dressed to the nines. It would upset me to no end. Who dresses like that for school?

To add insult to injury, she took me to the doctor when I was just sixteen to get breast implants. It was her idea. I thought my breasts were just fine. I was sixteen years old with a C cup. I had beautiful, youthful teenager boobs. But this doctor was somewhat of a local celebrity. He judged all the big national swimsuit competitions and pageants. So, I thought, he must know what he's talking about, right? I trusted him implicitly. But I was also always in great physical shape. Nevertheless, my grandmother told the doctor to do it anyway. She said it was just a good thing to do. I went along with it. *Why not?*

But I didn't realize at the time that she wanted to control me completely. I was too busy with my studies to fully understand her motives at the time. She wanted me to get into swimsuit modeling. It made her feel important. She wanted to "show me off," to brag about me to everyone she met. On one hand, it was flattering, but even at the time, I remember thinking it was a little strange and obsessive. It wasn't until years later that I truly understood her motives and the mental struggles she dealt with. I became her identity, and as long as people fawned over me as she bragged about my looks and my achievements, they were indirectly also praising her. Her abuse was mental, emotional, and in its own way, physical.

I continued to excel in college. I had virtually no contact with my mother throughout college, and certainly not my father. There were a few times that my father called to ask me for signed copies of my swimsuit calendars so he could give them to his buddies at the body shop in Hyattsville where they all worked, but that was the extent of it. I did invite both of them to my college graduation party and they both showed up, ironically. Looking back, though, I'm sure it was more about the open bar and the fact that they wanted to see each other more than they wanted to see me. Nevertheless, it was one of the proudest days of my life when I walked across the stage to accept my diploma. I splurged a little and threw myself a party on campus. I had it catered and hired a DJ. This was no dorm room kegger. The guests wore fancy cocktail party attire and the party was sophisticated. It was to celebrate my achievements. I made it! And I wanted to prove to the world that I did it!

I rented a house at the beach in Ocean City with my friend Tina after I took the GED and before I started classes at the University of Maryland. It was a little pink house just a few blocks from the beach. I did the bikini contest circuit all summer to pay my rent, car payment, bills, etc. I made lots of money doing those contests. Miss Hawaiian Tropic, Miss Venus Swimwear, Best Body on the Beach, were just a few of the pageants I participated in and won. My breast implants were certainly paying off! I never regretted getting them. I belonged to a gym called OC Sneakers, which is where I met Kent. He worked there. I was shooting around on the basketball court when he walked over and introduced himself. I think he was surprised that I was proficient in the sport. That's what happens when you grow up in Prince George's County! It was practically a requirement to know how to shoot hoops. There weren't many tennis courts to be found around town, but there was a basketball court in every neighborhood. Kent played basketball in college so I think he was a little impressed with my skills, even though he acted as if he didn't notice. He was very tall and had a great muscular build, and even as a young man, he had a quiet, commanding presence about him. He was solid to the core; he had morals, values, and character. Kent was never one who was easily influenced by others, nor did he care what other people thought. He would help his friends move in a New York minute; he would hold doors open for men and women alike and whether they thanked him or not; and he would frequently step up to an elderly shopper at the supermarket to help them load groceries into their cars. These traits are hard to find in mature adults, much less young people. I remember a time when my lifelong friend and her husband were having some financial difficulties. They were very worried about the bills, especially their mortgage. One evening during dinner I told Kent how worried I was for my friend, that she and her husband were in danger of losing their house. A few days later, my friend called to tell me that there was an envelope in her mailbox with a few thousand dollars in it. There was no note. She was in tears...beside herself and so grateful for this unexpected gift. She couldn't even believe it! I didn't tell her, but I knew instantly that it was from Kent. The fact that he treated my friends as my family was the best gift he could have given me.

We became friends. And although we might have kissed once or twice, our friendship was strictly platonic. I wasn't ready for romance, but we sure had a great time with each other. He worked at a local bar called the Angler, as a bouncer, and let me and my friends sneak in. I'm sure he could have gotten fired if his bosses found out. I adored Kent, and he was always so respectful of me. He never pressured me to do anything or go anywhere I didn't want to. We loved going to this little local diner. It was called Layton's, and we'd go there late at night and chow down on some eggs and toast. That was our thing.

The person I did have a relationship with was Jake. We met at the Cellar, which was a bar on the University of Maryland campus. I was just sixteen and he was twenty-one and we met on the dance floor. He was a great dancer. We just hit it off. We had the same rhythm; we were in sync with each other. He was the BMOC (Big Man on Campus), and larger than life. And true to all guys all over the world like him, all the guys wanted to be like him and all the girls wanted to date him. We dated for a few years. He was five years older than I was. . .very hot, very charming, and such a risk-taker. He wasn't a bad boy to the extent of hurting anyone or being mean-spirited, he just liked the adrenaline rush of doing risky things.

He enjoyed living on the edge. He went to "fast" parties and D.C. dance clubs that were a little "dark" or forbidden. He, along with some of his football buddies, were hoping to be recruited by the NFL and CFL. As a result, they thought they were larger than life and partied like rock stars.

One night after a game, the whole team reveled in victory against its main rival. The fans were cheering and running onto the field, and the perky fan girls swarmed Jake. "Oh my God, you were so amazing," squealed a tall brunette with blue eyes and freckles. She leaned in close to kiss him on the cheek. He smiled and turned to some kids who were offering up jerseys for his autograph.

Jake loved the attention, and he also knew how to work the crowd.

"Hey, if you aren't busy later, you want to get something to eat?" the brunette continued.

"Or how about a drink?" purred a curvy blonde. "You must be thirsty after such a rough game!"

"Oh ladies, you flatter me! And as much as I'd love to, I have a girlfriend." But that didn't stop him from winking at them and flirting a little. *Who wouldn't love the adoration?*

In spite of the fact that I swore I would never date someone like Jake, someone so opposite my style and too much of a risk-taker, my heart won out. He'd pursued me with reckless abandon and did everything right. He was charming and chivalrous. Jake was not disingenuous. He wasn't just trying to score. We fell in love and had one of the most passionate relationships I'd had in my young life. But deep down I knew it wouldn't last. I was attracted to "safe," stable guys, and Jake was the opposite of all this. But I'm so grateful we had the relationship we had. He introduced me to the thrill of risk-taking, but he also helped me confirm in my heart and in my head that my life was not one that I wanted to expose to wild risks. Calculated ones, fine. But I swore then, and still do now, that I'll fight to the death to keep my life and my loved ones safe from those who want to inject a little too much risk where it's not wanted or welcomed.

I was only attracted to risk if it could potentially better my life. I never took typical "teenager" risks. I never drank or tried drugs, ever. Never tried a cigarette. Those risks would not better me (or anyone in my opinion). I had no desire to follow the crowd. I had zero tolerance for "weak" people. Get a backbone! Stand up for what you believe in! Don't cower. People who fell for these traps were so unattractive to me. Even though I was still a teenager, I was much too strong for that. Too determined. I had too much on the line to get involved with that petty stuff. The risks I took were about survival. And about breaking the vicious, abusive cycle that my mother and grandmother tried to keep me in. No matter what, I had to survive by my terms.

I did learn a lot from Jake, though. And I always think fondly of him for helping to bring me out of my safe zone. I learned that calculated risks can be beneficial and that sometimes, spontaneity was the key to growth.

Because of my upbringing, it was hard for me to look outside of my carefully orchestrated life. Every semester, my classes were meticulously planned out so I could graduate as quickly as possible and move on from this place and all that it represented. I made some time for recreation, but nothing so time-consuming that it would delay my progress.

One night, we went to our favorite local restaurant, Jasper's. It was a casual but upscale local restaurant with high, glossy, marine-varnished tables surrounded by barstools. Pendant lighting peppered the ceiling and the bar was center stage with probably 150 sparkling lead crystal bottles. Modern art by local artists hung on the walls, illuminated by museum-style spotlights. The atmosphere was always lively and patrons got to know each other at the shared tables.

Our favorite appetizer was the crab dip. Maryland is famous for its crab, and there was no shortage of this delicacy in the dip. We loved it so much we never ordered anything else. The crabmeat was sweet and plentiful, mixed in with spices and super melty cheese. We always fought over the homemade fried tortillas and sliced French bread that accompanied the dip and sometimes would even place two orders.

As we tucked into the bubbling platter of dreamy deliciousness and tried not to scald our mouths on the cheesy, liquid lava, Jake mentioned out of the blue that it was always one of his biggest dreams to go to Hawaii, where his ancestors were from. His parents always spoke fondly of their families and the beautiful landscape. We both started daydreaming about the islands and ended our evening with full bellies and dreams of making it there one day.

"How was your date?" my grandmother asked.

She rarely took interest in my activities unless they were beauty pageants or photo shoots. I was immediately suspicious.

"It was fine. We had crab dip at Jasper's," I replied. I looked at her face, her expression, anything that might reveal the true reason for her interest.

"Did you know Jake's ancestors are from Hawaii?" I asked. I was hoping a change of topic might bore her into going to bed and leaving me alone.

"Oh Bridgette, I had no idea! How exotic!"

It was the most interest she'd taken in my life since I got my breast implants. I know she adored Jake—that was no secret. She watched every one of his games on television and made no secret of her overwhelming desire that our relationship become more serious.

A few days later, a card appeared on the dining room table with my name written in cursive on its front. I opened it to find a pair of airline tickets to Hawaii. Not only that, a printed confirmation for a seven-day upscale hotel also inhabited the envelope.

She was watching me as I opened the card and discovered its contents. I didn't even notice her hovering.

"Bridgette, you and Jake should take some time to enjoy yourselves," she started, in a too-sweet voice.

"Um, uh, what. . ." I stuttered.

"You both work so hard. Go on. It's his dream, right? His family is from the islands? Won't he be excited?" she gushed.

And in a déjà vu moment, I remembered the day she took me to a high-end medical building. The look on her face then was the same one that greeted me now. It was a mixture of jealousy, glee, narcissism, and. . .control. And once again, I had no idea where she got the money.

I was hesitant to go. Hesitant to even mention it to Jake. But the next time he came over to pick me up for a date, my grandmother greeted him at the door and ruined my plans.

"Jake! It's so good to see you!" she started.

Over the next few minutes, I tried to distract her and get her away from him, but I failed. She planned out her reveal with steely precision. As she unleashed the news, Jake's face practically glowed with joy and excitement.

He looked from my grandmother to me, then back again.

I blinked. I didn't know what to say.

"Bridge? You're excited, right?" he asked, not knowing whether to smile or not.

"Um," I started. . .there were so many things to consider. . . paying her back, rescheduling my classes, getting notes from classmates for anything I'd missed while I was gone. The fact that I hadn't told him immediately.

"Um, I can't. I have classes," I said, my heart dropping.

"Nonsense. You're at the top of all your classes. Tell your teachers someone died. It'll be fun. Live a little!" he said, his eyes twinkling as he smiled at me. "Honey, we can watch the NFL draft from Hawaii! Come on. Please."

Ten days later, I found myself leaving on a jet plane.

Oahu was a world away from Prince George's County. I'd traveled to compete in contests, but never as a vacation. Work and competing was always involved. I wasn't accustomed to just going to a fancy place to just. . .vacation.

I felt like a princess the minute we got off the plane. We were met by organizers who draped fragrant leis around our necks and escorted us to waiting cars that swept us off to the resort hotel. It took a few hours before I stopped fretting about school and just gave in to the experience. Jake and I woke up early to watch the NFL draft from our five-star resort on Oahu. He had a few friends who were drafted and these were very exciting times for him. (Jake went on to play in the CFL for a brief period of time before moving on to arena football. I was so very proud of him.)

When we weren't glued to the draft results, we busied ourselves with suntanning on the beautiful beaches, shopping, and just being two carefree college kids living in a dream. There were so many happy vacationers that I could either talk with them or just people watch. It was an amazing experience to be able to just let go and be free.

I ate poi for the first time and learned about island culture through its cuisine. We went to a luau and ate succulent roast pig with crispy skin and fresh pineapple dripping with juice. The sunny weather and cool breezes calmed our city souls and gave us both a feeling of oneness with the Earth. Touring volcanic ridges reminded us that Mother Nature is much more powerful and all-consuming than any minute problems we think we might have, and it was a profound lesson to learn. Our seven days felt like a month (in a good way) and I was so sad to see it pass so quickly.

What surprised me the most about the experience was that when we returned home, nothing catastrophic happened. My classes went on as normal. Campus was normal. I didn't miss anything life changing. I learned to let my hair down a little and not be so worried about life. Maybe I could relax just a little bit from time to time after all.

Thank you, Jake, wherever you are, for sharing one of your dreams with me.

CHAPTER 10

A Little Song,

a Little Dance

It was a Saturday night and the restaurant was packed. This was the peak time for business and the kitchen and bar buzzed with food and drink orders from frenzied waitstaff. Diners relaxed at linen-covered tables with real cloth napkins folded into pleated fans and nestled in crystal flutes. The place settings boasted fancy china, two forks along with a knife and spoon, and a bread plate. Our menu offered center-cut filet mignon grilled in butter to a perfect medium rare and topped with micro greens; yellowtail Hamachi with jalapeno and chili oil; beef carpaccio; glistening bone-in New York strip steak, and thick-cut veal chops. It definitely wasn't vegetarian-friendly. Our clientele included wealthy businessmen and celebrities. No riffraff.

The bar stretched thirty feet long and people opting for a liquid meal lounged on tufted leather chairs while the hot cowboy-in-the-city bartender turned out crafted cocktails with the same ease as pouring a scotch. Neat. This was no old-school, dingy bar attended by slovenly mid-level office managers drinking their problems away. The beveled mirror backsplash featured blue track lighting that gave the back bar a spooky, yet futuristic glow that showed off the crystal liquor bottles that contained the best in whatever devil's water could wet your whistle.

I worked there for about a year when I was nineteen and earned my college tuition and living expenses (as well as my grandmother's rent and food expenses) by squirreling away every red cent I earned. I wasn't a waitress or a bartender.

The venue also featured a chest-high platform stage.

With steel poles embedded from stage floor to ceiling.

And mirrored walls with dizzying disco lights swirling above.

The venue was called Scores.

And I was a Scores girl.

This job was my little secret. No one knew me in New York City. I worked a total of six weekends in the year I was there and I made enough money to pay all of my tuition. Girls could make thousands of dollars a night. It was insane.

§

While I was growing up, I was always active in cheerleading, basketball, figure skating, and sports in general. I loved physical activity and I had a slender, athletic build. But after I became estranged from my mom and my granddad died, my grandmother became obsessed with me. It's as if a light switched on in her head and she became a stage mother.

"Bridgette, come with me," she said one day, out of the blue. I was sixteen years old.

"Um, where are we going?" I asked. I wasn't scared, but rather confused because we never went anywhere together and I did my best to avoid interacting with her at all costs. It just made life easier.

"To the doctor. Now stop asking so many questions," she barked.

On our drive to the doctor, she was silent. Not in a frightened way, but in a smug, self-satisfied way. We headed for the ritzy part of town and I began to wonder if she was dying and going to see some expensive specialist in a last-ditch effort to save her life.

We parked and walked inside an elegant building with no signs or identifying marks. The elevators silently swept us up eight floors in a matter of seconds and opened onto a lobby that looked like Miranda's sleek, white office in *The Devil Wears Prada*.

"Hello," the model-thin receptionist said as we approached her frosted glass desk. On it was a telephone, a vase of fresh flowers, and an appointment book. "Name?"

I was looking at the waiting room and the patients in it. *They don't look very sick*, I thought. I shrugged it off, concluding to myself that they were waiting for family members.

"Bridgette? Come with me," a disconnected voice came from my left. I was knocked out of my thoughts as I turned toward the voice that summoned me.

"Wait, what?" I stammered. I looked back to my grandmother only to find her already in a nearby chair and picking up *Glamour* magazine. She didn't even look at me as I was led into the examining room.

What happened next I still can't fully believe. The doctor greeted me and informed me that my grandmother requested that I have cosmetic surgery. I remember seeing an interview with Donny Osmond when he shared with the world that, although he loved his parents for forever with all his heart, he could never put his *own* children onstage as mere toddlers and demand that they perform. That's how I felt in that doctor's office. I could never put my daughter in that situation. It's incomprehensible. And yet, there I was.

"What size would you like?" he asked clinically as he extracted implant samples from a cabinet behind his desk. "So, you want to be a model? I would advise a large 'C' cup. Nothing too big."

He then proceeded to mark my breasts with a Sharpie. It was the first time I'd been naked in front of a stranger and I felt paralyzed. Numb.

At that moment, I came to understand with soul-stripping clarity that my own grandmother was trying to objectify me for her own gain. My Sweet Sixteen "party" was getting a boob job. Apparently, my own flesh and blood grandparent wanted me to be a model and bring home the bacon. First it was my granddad, and now me. I also realized that there was no way this procedure would be covered by insurance unless there was a health-based reason. So somehow, my grandmother was footing the bill with. . .what? Money she should have used to pay the rent? Money she should have used to spruce up her home and make it comfortable and safe?

But there was little I could do to fight something that was not my decision. Unlike my battle for emancipation where I could prove what I had to prove for my own health and safety, the lines here were blurred. This doctor, as with so many like him, didn't care that I was underage. All he cared about was his bottom line. He was a very well-known plastic surgeon. He was good-looking, well dressed, and had an infectious bedside manner. He was a judge for all of the big national pageants and took an interest in me as a future contender. He sang my praises in the office and told me how much I would absolutely love my new boobs and that all the swimsuit models had them. He told me that I was beautiful and could win all of those pageants, hands down.

Post-surgery, I was very tender and had to be careful with how I moved around other people and within my surroundings. Any jarring or sudden movements could sometimes feel as if I was being stabbed. Or at least what I imagine being stabbed must feel like. Sometimes I'd even feel shooting pin pricks around the operation sites, almost like the phantom pains that amputees experience. But in spite of my discomfort, I have to admit, I loved my new boobs, almost to the point where I forgave my grandmother.

On a sunny spring morning about three months after the surgeries, I sat in the noonday sun in the campus quad while I read the *Diamondback*, which was the University of Maryland's campus newspaper. I'd usually only read the features and campus news sections, and I'd always check the student discounts section to see if I could save some money on groceries or the movies. But that day, I wasn't in a rush to get to class and read the newspaper from front to back. On the very last page, my eyes fell on an ad for a bikini contest where the winner would take home $5,000.

And that's when it clicked. It was time to use what I had to *my* advantage and not others' gain. Why not take advantage of the fact that men enjoyed looking at beautiful women in bikinis *and* make money at the same time? I saw nothing wrong with that idea. None whatsoever.

I entered that contest. And I won. It was the first of several that I would win throughout college: I went on to win Miss Hawaiian Tropic, Miss Venus Swimwear, and Miss Georgetown, among others. I won all the local contests, which led to national and international competitions. As the winner of these contests, my travel expenses were totally paid for by the sponsors. Miss Venus Swimwear took me to Florida, and I traveled to Hawaii for the Miss Hawaiian Tropic International competition. Having lived in the Washington, D.C., area all my life, I was more than used to harsh winters that lasted five months out of every twelve and unpredictable storms, snowstorms, and sudden arctic nor'easter wind gusts could take off a layer of skin that wasn't protected under a parka. It was such a treat to visit warm climates where I could wear sundresses and flip-flops or lounge around in a bikini and a sarong under a palm tree with a virgin piña colada at my side. It was all so unbelievably dreamy. Fandom, feeling beautiful and powerful and getting to travel the world for free? *What's not to love?*

The apex of my pageant life happened when a *Playboy* scout saw me compete and selected me to appear in the magazine. I got the once-in-a-lifetime chance to fly to St. Maarten for the photo shoot. In addition to competing on the pageant circuit, I also modeled for multiple swimsuit calendars during all four years of college. It was certainly a challenge to juggle the traveling, competing, and full-time college schedule. But I got to travel the world for free. I made good money. And most importantly, I was empowered by the liberation that self-sufficiency offered. I never felt any shame, then or now, about my competition and modeling years—or my time at Scores. Long after those days were over, I read that Bettie Page, the iconic poster girl from the 1950s, called her photo shoots "posing," and that she never felt ashamed despite the uproar from middle America that she was a tramp and a deviant. People will always judge others, but that doesn't always mean they're right.

Cheerleading was never far away from my thoughts or my eventual reality. During college, I competed against 400 other girls for a spot on the Washington Redskinettes cheerleading squad. I was beyond excited to not only make the team but I was also selected to be a member of the travel performing squad. The traveling squad was comprised of a select number of girls who had superior dance talent. It was an extremely elite, prestigious group of girls that performed at high-end events and for the U.S. troops.

Maybe you've heard the old adage that you've got to take the good with the bad. In my case, the good parts were the pageants, the travel, the liberation, and the self-sufficiency. No one can ever take those experiences away from me.

But there's a dark side too. And no one can ever take *those* experiences away from me either.

When people think about sex workers, they instantly think of call girls and adult film actors. But the term is much more widespread than the obvious. Think about it. Sex therapists could even fall under this umbrella. Men and women who charge clients for nonsexual cuddling or hugging sessions could be considered sex workers. Leggy models in skimpy dresses who pass around promotional flyers at trade shows in

Vegas could fall in this spectrum. The bottom line is, you're using sex—whether it's the actual act or a suggestion of the act—to elicit gains.

When I worked as a dancer, I absolutely *hated* it with every cell of my body and mind. Being so exposed was the worst feeling in the world. It made me sick.

Now don't get me wrong. I'm not a prude. I never minded performing on stage—a little show, a little dance. Everyone on the planet has some show-off tendencies in them. And there was space between me and the guys at my feet. No touching. No talking. Just a little seductive dance. I knew they wanted more but they couldn't have it. Sure, I could do that. I was the actress and the men were my audience. To my mind, it wasn't really that different from a bikini contest.

It was the lap dances that made me sick. They were too close for comfort. I didn't want to talk to these men, many of whom were very powerful and famous. We frequently saw movie stars, actors, and models streaming in and out of the club with their entourages of hangers-on. I didn't care what they had to offer. I did my act. I was there to do a performance and that's all.

"Hey beautiful," one guy slurred at me as I started my set.

He was easy on the eyes: slicked-back brunette hair, green eyes, a tailored suit from Brooks Brothers, and a silk shirt.

I ignored him and kept on dancing.

"Hey baby, wanna go someplace more private?" He was drunk.

I barely looked at him. For him and all the other men around me, I danced, gave them a little seductive show, and ran backstage at the end of my set to change for my next "show." There was nothing romantic or real about these performances. We dressed in custom-made dresses, sparkly jewelry, and stiletto heels, and even delighted in the artistry of backstage makeup artists, hairdressers, and seamstresses. A quick change, a few sprays of nice perfume and I was on to my next performance. You could even consider what I did there as a form of musical theater. I knew what my role was and I knew what the audience's role was; and never the twain shall meet. And unlike other venues, this club had top-notch security. Its performers were as protected as they could be. But that didn't stop customers from trying to take advantage of us.

"Honey, I've got a Maybach sitting outside. Let's go to Paris. Tonight," he said as he reached for my ankle. I kept on dancing and eventually moved to another portion of the stage. I kept an eye on him for the rest of my shift and witnessed him feeding the same tired lines to any woman who came within earshot. Sometimes I didn't know who I pitied more, the men or the women.

I was one of the lucky ones. Many of my co-workers were not. These girls were lured by the big shots, their money, their fame. Some people you could tell the money or fame was authentic. Others were just flashing cash before they headed out to return their father's old BMW to the garage before the old man found out.

So many of the girls were beautiful but naive, and many of them fell into a dark, lonely lifestyle because of it. The expectations, the promises, the dashed hopes again and again eventually wore down their resolve, their passion for life, and their self-esteem.

Drugs and alcohol didn't help, either. Many of the dancers were constantly stoned or drunk, and because of my own experience, I'd seen enough to last my lifetime and ones beyond. They were easily compromised; beautiful girls with no education, nothing to show for their lives, got mixed up with drugs and rich men who were only out for short-term fun.

I had a co-worker named Carla who seemed like a very sweet, down-to-earth girl. She was two years older than me and came from Arizona. Carla started around the same time I did and we often shared the stage or had back-to-back shifts. The club hired her because she was a former model and looked like she could be a movie star. As the weeks wore on, I started seeing her less and less.

"Heya," my boss started.

"Yeah? I can't really talk, I'm about to go on," I replied.

"When you see 'VIP room' tell her I need to talk to her."

He looked at me as if he expected me to know what he meant.

"What. . .who?" I asked.

"You know, the chick with the red hair, from Arizona."

"Carla? You mean Carla? Why do you call her 'VIP room'?" I was completely confused.

"What are you, blind? She spends all night in there. Anyhoo, tell her to come see me." And he walked away.

I didn't see Carla that night but I did run into her a few weeks later in our dressing room. I caught her stuffing a beer can-width roll of cash into her purse.

She said nothing as she zipped her purse and grabbed her coat.

"The boss wants to see you," I started, realizing immediately that she surely would have seen him since he first asked me to look for her.

"Sure he does. Probably wants some of my action," she said, and she flipped me off without looking back.

I never even saw the inside of the VIP room. I never witnessed what went on inside. I didn't have to. Doors close and are closed for a reason. Was there sex? Drugs? Arms deals? I'll never know, and I don't want to know.

And the pitiful sadness went both ways. We'd often see men who thought cash and fame could erase their bad attitudes, behavior, and personalities. On the other end of the spectrum were men who were socially awkward, afraid, or suffering from mental imbalances. These patrons thought that girls who were way out of their leagues were actually interested in them.

My time dancing was my own game to play and I was calling the shots. It may have been my riskiest move since I divorced my mother, but I was working the system and not letting it work me. And I had the support of one of the most important people in my life.

Kent.

I didn't tell him for a long time about Scores. I was so nervous. I didn't want him to think less of me. I remember telling him one day that I wanted to share something with him.

I looked into his eyes and felt weak.

"Of course! You know you can tell me anything," he assured me gently.

My heart was racing. I was scared I'd lose him. But I knew that I could not continue our relationship if a lie stood between us.

So, I did it. I revealed my big secret. I carefully watched the expression on his face. . .so afraid that he would be disappointed in me. . .but he barely flinched. He knew who I was and there was zero judgment from him.

Zero.

Kent was my biggest fan. He was unwavering. And never, not one time, would he ever let other people influence his own beliefs. He knew how mentally strong I was and knew it was a means to an end.

He said, "Bridge, you do what you have to do. The only person you have to answer to is YOU."

This man who had remained my dear friend despite my romantic dalliances with other men. . .the man who would become my husband and the father of my children. . .showed me his character early on. His kindness and unconditional love made me feel nurtured, cared for, and secure. Kent gave me something no one else ever had: he gave me his heart fully and completely. And with him in my life, I never looked back again.

BRIDGETTE PEARCE

CHAPTER 11

Yes and No

"Hey Bridgette," the disconnected voice came from behind me.

It was all at once familiar, yet strange.

I was used to having strangers approach me to get my autograph or snap a picture if they'd seen or owned one of my calendars, so that's what I initially thought on a warm summer day in my senior year of college.

I was out with my girlfriends at the beach and we'd stopped at this vibrant little bodega. It was a popular waterfront restaurant and bar, with rafts in the bay and tables under palm trees. Caribbean-inspired food like conch fritters and fried plantains as well as refreshing, fruit-laden tropical drinks. They had the best banana smoothies. I think most patrons enjoyed their frozen drinks spiked, but mine were always virgin.

The lazy afternoon was perfect for Arnold Palmers and a giant platter of appetizers that included meat pies, fresh papaya, and coconut rice with peas and ground beef. My travels certainly expanded my palate, one that had once been limited to canned foods and mass-produced sweets. In Hawaii, I developed an appreciation for fresh fish and tropical fruit. In California, fish tacos with *queso fresco*, shredded cabbage, salsa, and a squeeze of lime enveloped in freshly made corn tortillas were the ultimate street food. And on this day, I remembered those travels and the *joie de vivre* I experienced.

Those were the days when we could eat anything and not gain an ounce. We were a little sunburned; we were wearing cutoff shorts and bikini tops and it took us a while to cool off. The feeling of camaraderie and not having to worry about school or homework or the normal nose-to-the-grindstone life I'd been living for years was almost overwhelming.

"Bridgette! It's me!" the voice came again. I recognized it.

It was Kent. I whirled around with utter happiness and gave him a bear hug. He engulfed me and I could smell his aftershave. I felt as if I'd come home.

"Hey stranger! I feel like I haven't seen you in ten years!" He laughed.

He held my hand playfully and kissed my cheek. I thought it was really touching that, although he was with his friends and I with mine, he showed no hesitancy or embarrassment at being affectionate with me. It was just the kind of guy he was: full of integrity, true to his feelings, and sincere. We talked for a bit and then parted, our friends tugging at us to resume our separate visits.

And it was at that moment that I realized he was going to be the man I married.

§

"Hey babe, let's go grab some beers and pizza," Jake yelled from the living room.

When we first started dating, he would drink socially but he had it under control. First in his mind was football, and a big part of that was keeping fit and healthy. When he wasn't in school or with me, he was in the gym.

"Aww honey, maybe another night. Why don't we just have a night in? I'll make burgers," I said, hoping he'd agree.

And he did.

In the beginning.

In the first few months of our relationship, these episodes were few and far between, but as we grew closer and more comfortable with each other, another side began to emerge. I guess he felt he didn't have to be on his best behavior now that he "had" me.

Jake's drinking and reckless behavior started to spiral out of control about a year into our relationship. He was frustrated with football and just wanted to have a good time with me and his friends. And sadly, because I didn't drink, the time we'd spend together grew shorter and shorter. We still loved each other and loved spending quality time together, but I could feel him pulling away a little.

Jake and I never talked about marriage; I guess we were in a love-rut. We were both still so young and it was a safe, secure feeling to be in the relationship we were in. I know I was pretty happy and didn't want to think long-term because I thought I'd be sixteen forever and there was always tomorrow to think about marriage and a family. My #1 goal was still to graduate early from college and start my life and career, so marriage was a thousand miles from my radar.

One Saturday night, I did agree to beer and pizza. Well, pizza and iced tea for me. As long as I got to drive home. Jake was thrilled, which surprised me. I thought he'd pout because he assumed my demand to drive was a direct stab at his inability to handle his liquor. All I wanted was for us to get home safely.

We arrived at the pizza parlor around eight o'clock. It was late enough for all the families and kids hyper on too much salt from the pizza and too much sugar from the sodas to have left but early enough before the potheads arrived to chow down on whatever munchies they could afford.

The beer started flowing. Jake liked his beer.

He loved it. He loved it just a little too much.

I had flashbacks of my mom. I knew I could not relive this all over again. Not with someone else. I couldn't...and that night, I told him so.

All Jake wanted to do was play professional football. He hoped for the NFL or CFL, and his backup plan was to become a sports agent. He was a phenomenal quarterback and extremely talented, very well respected in the sports arena. However, he always thought his height was a deterrent. He was barely six feet tall. He eventually went on to play arena football and proved himself as an incredible athlete. But in those days, he also liked to party. Hard. And often. And that was what did us in.

DETACHED

A few nights later, I was at my friend Jessica's house when there was a knock on the door. Jessica opened it and Jake was standing there.

"Bridgette, I love you," he started.
"Um, I love you too, Jake. Are you OK?"

What happened next was one of the most surreal moments of my life. Everyone has seen home videos, movies, and real-life wedding proposals where the guy gets on one knee and the woman instantly claps her hands over her nose and mouth. And how many times do you think the viewer's reaction has been: *Why is this such a surprise? How could she not have known?*

I'm here to tell you that it WAS a surprise, and it was the furthest thing from my mind.

I saw Jake's mouth moving but it was like a badly captioned movie. I heard what he said with a three-second delay and my ears started ringing. He pulled the ring from his pocket and slowly moved toward me.

"Baby, I love you so much. Will you marry me?" he asked as he locked his eyes on me.

"Um. . ." I stammered.

In the next second, I began to feel nauseous, as if the weight of the world landed on my shoulders. I was face-to-face with the man I loved and he was proposing to me this very moment in time and all I could think of was how I wanted to be anywhere but here.

"Uh, Jake," I continued.

"Honey, I'm so sorry it happened here. I wanted to take you to some fancy restaurant and have a violinist, but I didn't want to spoil the surprise," he started.

"Jake, I love you so much. I just can't marry you," I said. My heart instantly broke into a million pieces, and I felt like I was suffocating. The reality of this heartbreak was different than any other I'd felt up to that point. It's the reality that he and I spent many years together and I did love him with all my heart. But the fact that he was starting to drink greater quantities of alcohol and more often—not just on a social level—was something I couldn't change. And when he got drunk, he took even more risks than he ever had before. When we were a new couple, he might speed a little on the highway for a few seconds or whisk me off to a show unannounced. But this risky behavior spiraled toward being downright unsafe, if not borderline illegal, the older he got and the more he lost control. These were risks I wasn't willing to be a part of, no matter how much my heart broke, and no matter how much I broke his heart.

I think the fact that he didn't hear the word "but" stalled his reaction.

All he heard was *Jake, love,* and *marry you.*

He tried to put the ring on my finger and kiss me.

"Jake, honey." By this time I was weeping.

And he finally saw that my tears were ones of despair and sadness.

Then Jake broke down and started crying. He asked for another chance. He promised to stop drinking so much. But I couldn't do it.

"Jake, I can't," I said gently.

He slowly got to his feet and walked to the door. He didn't look back. Once he got to his car outside, I peeked out the window and cried and cried for what could have been.

Jake was the traditional college relationship that I'm sure many young adults have. And he was so different than Kent.

When I was working in the clubs to pay my tuition, Kent knew all about it. All he cared about was my safety. The rest of it, to him, was a means to an end and he understood my motives. He respected them. We'd been platonic friends for what seemed like forever. We knew each other when I was with Jake, so when Jake and I broke up, it was a natural progression for Kent to be there and support me.

"Bridgette, why don't you come over and we can go grab a bite to eat. You can just do your homework over here," Kent offered.

"OK. I won't be in the way?" I asked.

He looked at me and smiled. It was a look that translated silently, *as if I didn't want you here, I wouldn't have asked.*

Kent had a roommate, Chris, whose girlfriend quickly became a dear friend and has remained so for more than twenty years. We were there for each other during the births of our children, and our children have been friends since birth. But at the very beginning, I had no idea that would be the case. When I got to Kent's town house, Chris and his girlfriend Aimee greeted me. I think they were both a little surprised to see me because Kent didn't typically introduce his dates to his friends. But this was different, and they knew that instantly. I could tell that Aimee was happy to have another woman around. Aimee was beautiful. . .she was tall and slender, blonde, with pretty blue eyes. She always had the best golden tan! She was—and always has been—sweet as can be. Aimee and I have always shared the same vision. We read the same books. We are both into self-motivation and becoming the best versions of ourselves. Our motto has always been "What you think about, you bring about."

Early in our friendship, we went to the beach with the guys for the annual New Year's Eve bash at Fager's. The DJ was playing the best dance songs! Aimee and I loved to dance. . . we danced the night away wearing our festive party hats and twirling our colorful noisemakers.

"Bridgette, they're playing "Baby Got Back"! Come on, let's dance!" Aimee shrieked as she grabbed my hand and jumped up and down. Her excitement and pure joy were infectious. It was that weekend that Aimee and I really started to bond. While the guys were chatting over beers, she and I would share our deepest thoughts and life goals and dreams during our "girl talk" sessions. Although she and Chris had been dating much longer than Kent and I, we were at the same stage in life: getting close to settling down and starting to think about marriage and kids.

Fast-forward to years later when Tye and Kolt were just toddlers. I met Aimee's baby girl, Kendall, for the first time when she was just a few days old.

Aimee was already back to her pre-pregnancy figure and looking as beautiful as ever! I always knew her as a totally put together, independent, vibrant woman, but I could tell as soon as I looked at Aimee that she was a deer in headlights.
"Bridge?" she said as we sat on the couch.

"Aimee, Kendall is such a calm baby!" I said as I looked at her little bundle of princess perfection cooing gently in her mother's arms.

"Bridge, oh my gosh, this is so hard! I don't know anything about being a mom!"

Aimee started to panic and her eyes filled with tears.

Becoming a mom for the first time was scary! I was no expert, but I already had two babies, so Aimee happily relied on me to give her new mom advice. We sat in her family room and chatted for about an hour. . .while I held sweet little Kendall. Aimee was beyond exhausted, so I knew I couldn't stay long. It was a deep, bonding experience that brought us closer than ever before. There's nothing like the bond between two close friends when they become moms for the first time.

Little did I know one of my closest friends would come from that invitation to the town house. I was a little hesitant because I didn't know what I was walking into, but my fears were quickly eradicated. The town house became my second home and the atmosphere was placid and accommodating.

Kent had recently earned his master's degree in finance and was already working as a financial advisor in a large downtown investment firm. In fact, he's still with the same company more than twenty-five years later.

He loved that he could help families prepare for their future. Loved that he could teach his clients how to live with a sense of security and peace and feeling of contentment. Of course there is always risk when dealing with other people's money—but the reward was much greater.

I graduated from UMCP soon thereafter with a bachelor of science degree. I was twenty-one. When I woke up on graduation morning, I was in a mood.

"I'm not walking," I said. The words sounded disconnected, unreal, as they came out of my mouth. Looking back, I don't know why I said them.

I busied myself with making breakfast and mechanically going about my morning routine as if it was any other normal day.

Yup, I'm not walking, I thought. I felt more adamant as I repeated it silently.

I turned from the stove to put the scrambled eggs on a plate and Kent stopped me in my tracks. He took the frying pan and set it back on the stove and gently grabbed my arms. He looked at me lovingly but with dead seriousness.

"Bridge, you are going to walk across that stage today and receive your diploma."

I looked at the ground. *No, I've made up my mind!*

He sensed my hesitation, but continued.

"Babe, look at me," he started. He jiggled my shoulders as if to shake me out of my thoughts.

"You are going to walk that procession today with your head held high and feel every bit of pride that you have earned. You deserve this moment and I'm not going to let you miss it."

I slowly raised my eyes to look at him.

Kent was right.

"Now go get your cap and gown and let's hit the road. If for no other reason, do it for me. *I* want to watch you walk across that stage. *I* want you to have this moment. I'm your biggest fan and more proud of you than you'll ever know."

He looked at me with determination and I felt nothing but love for him and renewed enthusiasm for what was about to come.

It wasn't the first—or last—time Kent pulled me out of my occasional worrisome thoughts. I was always driven and generally a positive person, but the ghost memories of my childhood always hovered in the background. Big life events triggered them, both then and even sometimes, now.

I couldn't believe the day was here. After all those years of hard work, focus, and sacrifice, I stood in line with my peers, ready to accept my diploma. I looked out onto a sea of black satin gowns and mortarboards with colorful tassels and heard the buzz of excitement and energy that came from the graduates. It felt electric.

As I walked the procession, my feelings were mixed. On one hand, I felt so incredibly proud and strong and intelligent. Not only was this an emotional and mental feeling, but a physical one as well. I felt as if I would explode out of my skin and launch right up into the sky, like you see action heroes do in the movies. The early afternoon sun shone on my face and I shut my eyes for a second. I felt confident and excited for the future. It was very surreal. And in that moment, a silly thought popped into my head.

I remember wondering if I should fling my cap into the air. For a second, I joyfully thought *Why not?* But then in the next second, I decided I'd worked so hard for this achievement and I didn't want to lose my cap. *What if I couldn't catch it? Would another classmate know or even care that it was mine and return it to me? What if I couldn't catch it in time and it got crushed in the crowd?* I pictured the opening to the old *Mary Tyler Moore Show* where Mary walked downtown and tore her red knit cap off her head to fling it in the air. She looked so happy and carefree, but I remember fretting every time I saw that clip. I wanted to remember this day forever and have mementos from it. The cap stayed firmly on my head.

But along with the feelings of pride and accomplishment, many deeper, darker feelings also surfaced. I felt embarrassed to walk across the stage with my family there. My uncles, aunts, and cousins came as well as my grandmother. . .but oddly enough, I don't remember if my mom was present. My dad was nowhere to be found. I didn't really feel a sense of loss. I barely knew them anymore. It was nice that they showed up, but I'm not really sure why they did. It's not as if we kept in touch. It's not like they really cared. Maybe they just wanted to see that I really did it. . .I don't know. The feeling was similar to having your sibling's neighbors show up at your wedding. You know them by association and have to be polite, but that's the extent of the interaction. You wouldn't miss them if they weren't there.

I remembered my determination to not walk the line. Just a few hours earlier, I was so bent on dumping the entire ceremony in favor of simply accepting my diploma privately and avoid the whole pomp and circumstance. But because Kent convinced me to walk, because he reminded me that it was important to live life as fully as possible and not have any regrets, I walked the procession and overcame those negative, intrusive feelings.

My graduation opened the doors to so many opportunities and I'd matured far beyond my years. Recruiters from companies in Los Angeles and New York that knew about my brief modeling career tried to convince me to work for them as a swimsuit model, I received offers to be on TV shows and to be part of big auditions, and I have to admit it was all very tempting. But ultimately, entertainment was not my dream. I'd worked too hard, survived too much, to not give something back to those who were in the same shoes I found myself in as a child.

Despite the temptation to take on a few high-paying gigs to put some money in a nest egg, I decided that after all my effort, it was the smart and prudent decision to pursue a more traditional career. I started working for the United Way in 1999. Initially I worked in public sector fundraising at the state level and worked my way up to the directorship of all public sector campaigns at the city, state, and federal levels. My work there was definitely my passion, but I guess I never really explained to my kids what my organization was all about. Recently, my son Kolt asked how I liked working for United Airlines when I was younger. Out of the mouths of babes.

Working for United Way was the absolute perfect career for me. It was my passion—my purpose. Every day when I woke up, I knew I was giving back to the community. Many days I was able to visit our member agencies to see where the dollars were going. To walk into a homeless shelter and watch a young mom receive job training and witness her adorable son get the opportunity to play in his soccer game with brand-new cleats; or witnessing a teen girl fighting for her life with Stage IV brain cancer and getting the best possible treatment from top-notch doctors; or see an elderly couple being taken to their doctors' appointments by a caretaker filled me with joy and pride.

You sometimes hear the adage that says something to the effect that "you meet the people you need the most in your life at the right time in your life in order to learn from them." I know this to be true, not just with people but with situations and opportunities. My mother, clearly, was the flashpoint, but over the years, Jake, Kent, my grandmother, my modeling and dancing opportunities, all of them offered chances for me to grow. During my time at UW, not only was the job perfectly suited to me, but so were the people—one in particular. The first time Carrie and I ever had a conversation was in her beautiful office, which was next to mine. Both were nicely furnished and spacious, with modern furniture and sleek desks. The ten-foot ceilings capped floor-to-ceiling windows that offered stunning views of Baltimore's inner harbor. They could have been featured in an ad for Baltimore.

We worked so hard for the organization and its cause because we believed in it wholeheartedly. And we enjoyed the perks of those efforts, too. When the Baltimore Ravens won the Super Bowl and the NFL parade worked its way through the streets of downtown, we watched it from our windows...we had the best seats in the house! Carrie and I shared a passion for giving back. We shared a strength...one that most women don't possess...one that empowers other women.

She was smart, beautiful, and incredibly driven, and we had an instant connection. To this day, Carrie is a force to be reckoned with, and is among the best in her field. Carrie managed the Tocqueville and Leadership Society and created the Women's Initiative in Baltimore. Carrie is a no-nonsense businesswoman. She has a heart of gold but the inner strength of an ox. She is relentless in her efforts to give back to the community because she cares deeply about the causes she supports. I admired her from day one. Not only is she amazing at what she does in her career, but she is one of the best moms I know: she truly is Wonder Woman. Carrie is not afraid to take smart risks or to voice her opinion even if it is the minority vote. She encompasses what women should be: strong, confident, independent, self-assured, resilient. What an incredible role model for her children and all those lucky enough to be in her orbit.

In 1998, Kent and I went to Clearwater Beach, Florida, for a little getaway. We visited friends, soaked up the sun on the beach, rented scooters and explored the town. It was relaxing and perfect. One night, he said we had plans to watch the dolphin show on the beach.

And I believed him.

As we walked along the shore, I noticed that there were no dolphins. There was no show. Only a table adorned with rose petals with two glasses of champagne and chocolate-covered strawberries. He got down on one knee...and I knew, right then and there, with every ounce of my soul, that this was to be my future husband.

I said yes.

My grandmother was beside herself when my relationship with Jake didn't work out. When she learned of Kent's proposal, she became very cold and distant toward me. She thought Kent was too "Wall Street". . .or a show-off. Little did she know that her perception couldn't have been further from the truth. Kent and I dated off and on during college. We got more serious as time went on. He was my very best friend. I knew, beyond a shadow of a doubt, that he was a part of my soul.

We got married the following year at Chapel by the Sea in Clearwater Beach. The building was finished in blindingly white plaster that reminded me of the cliffside structures in Santorini, Greece. The terra-cotta Spanish tile roof softened the stark white building, which was surrounded by majestic date palm trees and tailored hedges. The sides and back of the church were embraced by a deep sun porch to shield guests from the blazing sun that reflected off the sand that led to the ocean. It was an ideal setting for our big day; we didn't want a non-event where we would elope, but we didn't want a pretentious soirée that our guests felt uncomfortable attending because there was a formal dress code and a grand, opulent, butler-attended reception. We wanted our guests to share our day in a casual, comfortable, friendly atmosphere.

And they did, but not before Mother Nature stepped in. We'd had great weather in the days leading up to the wedding, but the night before, the skies blew open and a monsoon hit. We were in the middle of our rehearsal dinner and were enjoying the balmy temps while we sat on the veranda. What started out as a gorgeous, warm evening eroded away as the winds kicked up. And not a moment too soon, the restaurant had to "roll down the plastic windows" before we were drenched by wind-driven, side-blasting rain. The wind was gusting by the time we moved inside, but we just chalked it up to good luck. A storm tonight would blow over by morning, as it frequently did in Florida.

"Bring it on! We got this!" Kent and I yelled at each other as the winds drowned out our voices.

The morning of my wedding day, I was in the hotel with my bridesmaids and the time came for each to visit the in-house hairdresser. When my friend Jess came back upstairs, she looked at me in the strangest way. I couldn't tell whether she was about to laugh or cry. And I wasn't sure if I was about to laugh or cry.

"Bridgette," she started.

All Jess needed to complete the look of a 1980s hairband singer was some black eyeliner, stonewash jeans, and a ripped sweatshirt.

"Jess, honey, you look uh. . ." I tried to squeak out.

I couldn't hold it in, and neither could the rest of my bridal party, Jess included.

"Do I look OK? I want you to be happy. . ." she started. She was such a trooper. "Bridge, you know I love you and I would do anything for you, but. . .I can't be seen in public like this. Walking through the lobby was bad enough, but at least those people were strangers and I'll never see them again!"

My sweet friend tried so hard to pretend that she liked the giant cotton candy hair sculpture on top of her head as we all finally broke down into peals of laughter.

"Jess, go get that hair fixed!" I squealed. My whole party was relieved, and the moment was priceless. We laugh about it even today. We named it Hairgate.

I went down to the lobby to tell the front desk that we were canceling the remaining hair appointments, and as I stepped off the elevator, I stopped dead in my tracks. My mother was checking in at the front desk. She was here.

In Florida.

At my wedding.

A million crazy thoughts sped through my mind as I ducked back into the elevator. Thank God she didn't see me; I wasn't prepared for this.

How did she get here? I didn't invite her. Who told her?

I was overcome with emotion and broke down in tears as I made my way back to the suite. I didn't know what to think or feel. I was angry. Pissed off. Sad. And...happy? I wasn't sure. Her presence threw me into a state of confusion, but I knew I wasn't going to let her ruin my day. I cried a few more tears, and my girls just thought I was releasing some stress. I didn't have the energy to get weighed down by telling them the whole story. I got myself pulled together and prepared myself for the reason I was here...my wedding.

DETACHED

I was ready.

The ceremony was beautiful. Kent's sister, Jennifer, was our soloist. Her voice. . .*wow*. It was heavenly, warm, and soulful. It took you to another place. What a lovely, perfect day. And it was followed by an almost perfect reception.

We hired a DJ that played old-school music, classic rock, and dance music. We all danced the night away and had so much fun. The party was a celebration of our love and the love we shared with lifelong friends. The older folks looked at us like we had four heads and spoke an alien language from Mars or something!

But, in addition to my mother's very presence at my wedding almost throwing me for a loop, so was her presence at the reception. As the night went merrily on, and the open bar wound down to a close. . .my mother approached the DJ.

I looked up with a little fear in my heart. As she took the microphone from him, I momentarily calmed down, thinking she was going to take that opportunity to give us a toast. I wondered what she would say.

There would be no toast.

Instead, she whispered a few unintelligible words to the DJ while she covered the mic with her hand. The feedback deafened us. Seconds later, the DJ started playing a rap song and my mother started rapping into the mic. Yes. *Rapping*.

That's just my baby's daddy. . .she started, a little off beat from the track that was playing behind her. *Was this a joke?*

And she continued, painfully...in front of me, in front of Kent, in front of all of our guests. It was difficult to watch and no one knew how to react. But thankfully, it ended before she could finish the entire song and the DJ was seasoned enough to switch gears and put on some dance music so the party could continue.

But, in spite of the weather, the hair debacle, and my mom's presence, it was a great day.

Kent and I settled into a happy life together. We took vacations, enjoyed dinners with friends, backyard cookouts, and business events. We discovered our favorite TV shows to watch together (even though he always fell asleep). We were both very family oriented and couldn't wait to have children of our own.

And as with everything else in our lives and between each other, we stayed true to our promises. Our two sons, Tye and Kolt, were born in 2001 and 2004, and our daughter Kennedy came along in 2006. With each pregnancy, Kent and I were over the moon! We had the same views on parenting. He supported my *Babywise* theory (a controversial book at the time). I was adamant about keeping my babies on a schedule. A strict schedule. Not everyone agreed with it, but my pediatrician said that my theory was completely healthy and fine. They ate every three hours—and not a moment before. I woke them (yes, I WOKE my sleeping baby) when it was time to eat... and I can tell you that my kids have been the very best sleepers since they were six weeks old.

My relationship with my mother, or lack thereof, had zero impact on my pregnancies or births. In fact, after my first child was born, I couldn't even fathom *not* having my sweet baby boy in my life until the day I died. I would walk through fire to get to my kids. I would swim the depths of the ocean to get to them. So if anything, I felt even more disconnected to my mother because I knew the ease in which she walked away from me. And even if it wasn't easy, she still allowed it to happen.

She still let her only child go.

How could she breathe? Without my children, I would have no oxygen. I didn't have any contact with my mother when I found out I was pregnant or when I gave birth to any of my children. If anything, I knew, beyond a shadow of a doubt, that she didn't deserve to be in their lives.

And so. . .

She wasn't.

BRIDGETTE PEARCE

CHAPTER 12

The Endless Circle

I looked out over my deck, which sits up high and overlooks my backyard and the trees and woods behind it. I could see the sun to my left as it set on the horizon to signal the Earth's tango step into the evening. The sky was always brilliantly red and orange and just so spectacular! Every morning on our drive to school, I would say to my kids, "Look at the beautiful sky!"

I was (and am) always in awe of the sky, whether the sun is rising or the sun is setting. In the mornings it is a beautiful combination of pinks and purples, and at night, the vibrant golds gave way to deep vermillion hues before shifting to a deep, inky blue.

Midnight blue.

I could look at the sky forever.

It takes me away.

It is my serenity.

Sitting in the stillness was a rare respite for me. And on this spring evening, the family was busy, but the ins and outs of their activities were quieted by the French doors. One of the doors opened onto the deck from the kitchen and breakfast nook. I'd catch glimpses of the kids as they moved about, each one yelling a muffled "Hi Mom" or "I'll see you later" from inside. I was glad for the connection.

§

I'd gone to dinner recently with some girlfriends and, as we ordered appetizers, I noticed a family sitting at a four-top across from us. The parents were middle-aged and the kids were teenagers. The mom had deep brunette hair that looked too perfect, its auburn halo a tip-off that she used hair dye with gray coverage. She had a French manicure and wore an expensive charm bracelet, and a Louis Vuitton Mahina satchel had been carelessly dropped on the floor. It reminded me of a photo of the late Carolyn Bessette Kennedy having coffee at a sidewalk café, her $20,000 Hermes Birkin stuffed to the gills as it rested on the concrete sidewalk. Wealthy women don't care where they put their expensive bags. Those who have saved up for them by eating Cup-a-Soup for a year set them on chairs and seat belt them in the car to keep them from falling into the footwells.

The dad wore khaki slacks, flip-flops, and a Batman T-shirt. And a Rolex submariner two-tone oyster-bracelet watch. Both kids were immersed in their phones, texting and checking out viral cat videos or Instagram. They didn't look particularly preppy or snobby; both wore jeans and T-shirts without any obvious labels.

DETACHED

I instantly reacted from a parent's perspective of *Oh, how rude is it that those kids are out for a family dinner and they're ignoring their parents!*

But then I noticed the parents were equally immersed in their phones. The mother was texting and the father was playing a video game. No one looked at each other. I didn't know if the kids were taking after their parents, the parents were just reacting to their teenagers' obsessions with social media, or if the family was so dysfunctional that being "connected" involved technology and not good old face-to-face interaction.

I was instantly reminded of the importance of unplugging—of spending a week, a day, even an hour off the grid. Turn off the TV, computer, and cell phone. Do a crossword puzzle. Read a book. Do some Mensa puzzles. Enjoy a meal with your loved ones. Have actual conversations with them. Doing so was one of the goals Kent and I had as parents: Don't lose the connection by being over-connected.

We'd worked very hard for our success and wanted to raise our children in a safe, secure, and balanced environment. We were (and are) very fortunate that all three of our kids are healthy, happy, and thoughtful young adults. They are good, solid kids. They are strong in their faith and values. Despite the normal challenges that all teenagers face, I believe they make wise choices most of the time. They respect themselves and each other. My kids have huge hearts.

I thought of their childhoods and the early physical challenges my boys had. Tye and Kolt both had pyloric stenosis and had surgery at two weeks old. Tye later had open heart surgery when he was just under two years old. I thought of my only daughter, as I was an only daughter to my mother. I thought of my childhood and how very different it was from theirs.

And I reached for my drink.

It was a glass of Shafer Chardonnay.

After my entire life of abstaining from things that could prove addictive, I allowed myself this one occasional vice.

Because I knew I was *not* my mother.

And in my mind and heart, I'd finally reached a place where I could thank my mother for making me the woman I'd become . . .instead of the woman I *could* have become.

§

"Bridgette, get me some coffee. . .I have a headache," my mother said, in as loud a voice as her pounding head would tolerate.

I was only eight years old. And by that age, I knew that "headache" meant my mother had a hangover from whatever she'd ingested the night before. I dutifully went to the kitchen and made some coffee, hoping it was all she'd ask for, and carried the coffee mug to her bedroom.

The sight before me was a familiar one. My mother, a talented hairstylist and otherwise physically healthy woman, lay half covered with moth-eaten blankets on a single mattress on the floor. She was dressed in an overly large T-shirt and her underwear even though it was freezing outside. The room had a bare lightbulb overhead. It was once covered with a frosted, fluted, Tiffany knock-off diffuser, but that had gone missing long ago . . . maybe sold for or traded for a fix. There were clothes all over the floor: some I recognized, some not. She reached out, searching blindly for the cup that she knew was near. She shielded her eyes with the other arm, and I noticed it was covered with fresh bruises.

All at once I felt shame, fear, desperation, anger, and frustration. And some regret. Regret that this adult woman, my mother, could not bring herself to rise out of the ashes of addiction and victimization. I don't know what caused her actions, her addiction, but I knew, even as a child, that she didn't see a way out of it. Maybe she did, but felt helpless to change.

§

If you asked me then what I thought life would bring, I don't know that I would have imagined that I would become the woman I have become with the family and lifestyle that I'm blessed with. What I did know by the time I was eight years old was that my life would be very different from my mother's life. Something inside my head dictated to me that I could make my own life, make my own choices, and that I could be proactive about it. I would do my best to not let my life be dependent on the choices and actions of others, that I would work to control as much as I could and be as successful as I could.

My mother, despite her faults, was not a lazy person, and I don't think had a mean bone in her body. But she made bad decisions and continues to live with the consequences of those decisions. I witnessed the impact of her decisions and knew I didn't have to follow in her footsteps. I could stop the cycle of bad choices, passivity, victimization, and addiction by traveling the opposite road that my mother took.

My children are what some people would call lucky because they were born into and raised in a loving home and enjoy a very comfortable lifestyle that Kent and I have provided for them. They attend prestigious private schools and they're growing up happy and healthy. I couldn't ask for smarter, kinder, more balanced kids, but because neither Kent nor I grew up in the surroundings and lifestyle that they're used to, it is my legacy to ensure that my children, this next generation, continue to uphold the cycle that I broke when I was a child.

Our collective efforts as parents were, among other things, to ensure that the lives of our children were better than the ones we had growing up. We've earned every drop of our success because of old-fashioned hard work, dedication, and drive. Kent and I made the decision that I should stay home and raise the kids once Kolt was born in order to support Kent's growing success. It no longer made sense for me to work outside of the home when I had two. . .and soon after, three babies to raise. Kent and I were a great team when it came to running our household. However, I always kept my foot in the door with local fundraising, events, and consulting. Giving back was my passion, always.

Life is not about money or cars or things you can show off; those are merely superficial material things that don't define a person's character. We have strived to raise our children to be loving, giving, devoted, and loyal people who, despite the social class that they live in, don't see color, nationality, religion, or any other distinction between them and those around them.

Tye, my eldest, is very intelligent by nature. He never has to study to do well in school, and has a business-centric mind that makes him really strong in math and the sciences.

DETACHED

"See ya, Mom," Tye said as he ran through the kitchen to grab some baby carrots and a protein bar before heading out for a quick workout at the gym.

At six feet three, he is athletic and plays at least one sport most seasons. Tye takes physical fitness and health very seriously.

"Honey, what about your homework?"

I heard his sneakers chirp on the tile as he stopped in his tracks.

"It's done. Just some econ. No big deal. Love you!"

And in a second, he was out the door. Another inch or two and he'd hit his head on the door frame. It made me remember marking the kids' heights on that door frame and made me a little teary. My eldest son was on the verge of entering college.

College.

How time flies. This remarkable human being grew up from a tiny baby who needed open heart surgery into a loving, intelligent, kind young man who has impeccable manners and a huge, giving, loving personality. Tye works as a camp counselor for children in the summer and oversees the middle school after-care program during the school year. One of his greatest strengths is his faith. He never forgets to say his prayers and thank God for his blessings. Tye and I have always had a special bond; maybe it was due to the closeness we shared after his open-heart surgery . . . when he was so fragile. I remember rocking him back and forth when he was barely two years old as we watched *Scooby-Doo*. I had to feed him a banana every single day so he would get enough potassium after his surgery. We talk about anything and everything, and I cherish our talks. I have no idea how I will be able to let him leave the nest and go off to college. I get a lump in my throat just thinking about it. . .my heart is heavy and yet, I'm so proud.

My second child and second son is Kolt. If he and Tye ran out the door at the same time, he would hit his head. At just fifteen years old, he's already over six feet five with no end in sight. He is an amazing basketball and football player in addition to being one of the best athletes on his teams. My son is also an honor roll student, but despite this combination of super achievement that might make most teenagers conceited and self-absorbed, Kolt is quiet, humble, and kind. And he's not afraid of hard work.

"Mom, I need some new cleats, please." I looked down at his feet and his ninety-day-old cleats that showed his big toe pushing against the leather toe-box like it was ready to burst. He'd grown at least one shoe size in three months, and an inch in height, too.

"Honey, please put it on the calendar, OK? We'll go this weekend. Just remind me," I said.

"But there's no room. . ." Kolt said, as he walked closer into the laundry room with our wall calendar. Each day was marked up with his schedule in blue, Tye's in green, and Kennedy's in red. Kolt's schedule usually starts with a pre-class workout at 6:00 a.m., then seven hours of class followed by basketball or football practice. Top this with his church group "Uprising," and it's a wonder he even has time to breathe. And despite this impossible-to-imagine schedule, my son is always the first one to help me unload groceries or ask me if I need help around the house. He is the Energizer Bunny.

DETACHED

Kennedy is my only daughter and the youngest, at thirteen. She is my sweet, beautiful princess and is athletic, just like her brothers (she plays basketball and tennis) but is also a girly girl. She is as competitive as her brothers, and also shares their sweet, loving demeanors and generous hearts.

"How do I look?" Kennedy asked one summery Saturday morning. I was drying my hair and didn't see her immediately. "Mom! I love this! Look, see?" she squealed.

I turned around to face my then twelve-year-old daughter to find her posing like a model in my bathroom. Here was my baby sporting jeans, calf-length Frye boots, and a white Free People jacket.

My Free People jacket. *My* Frye boots.

"How do I look, Mom? I'm so glad we can share!" she said, lowering her voice as she made fish lips and clasped her long hair on top of her head. We both burst out laughing. I'm so fortunate that she loves to talk with me in the car to and from school, and that we can talk about anything. Kennedy has a quiet demeanor...she goes to most of the boys' sporting events and never complains. She is so incredibly kind and would do anything for her brothers. She is not affected by what others think and is her own person with her own thoughts and opinions. She is confident, strong, and comfortable in her own skin. She loves fashion and shopping and mascara and pink lip gloss. There's just no one quite like her...my baby girl. *My* girl.

I do not want any of my children to take their lives or their lifestyle for granted, and as parents we continually instill in them the importance of knowing that there are always people who are both better off than they are and also less fortunate than they are. These facts sometimes get lost on children of privilege because they live in a bubble...they live in a very protected world where the realities of life are not always visible.

Kolt regularly travels to the inner city to play on a basketball team with other talented players from all walks of life. The joy he experiences from the camaraderie he has with his teammates is infectious. Every year on Christmas Eve morning, Kent and all three of my kids work in the city to deliver food to families in need. Many of the homes are filled with joy and love despite their difficult circumstances. These families are so incredibly grateful for the kindness shown to them. Some live tiny paycheck to tiny paycheck, and many have no income at all. They count their blessings very differently than we do. They don't take much for granted. Family is all they have. They make the sacrifices they have to make to ensure their families have the love and support they need.

And while I am so proud of the young adults my children have become, their goodness has also made me look closer at the families they serve. Witnessing their lives and struggles made me realize further that my mother could have made things work for us, but she chose not to. She was not (and will never be) the first or only person to ever suffer from life's challenges. Our children have met their grandmother but are not active parts of her life because she is not an active part of *theirs*. I remember a profound Stephen Covey quote that was printed, framed, and hung on the wall when I worked at United Way, *"I am not a product of my circumstances. I am a product of my decisions."* It sums up my mother's experience in spades. As she is living with her addiction and in the surroundings she's in to this day, I have to remind myself that these are her choices and no one else's.

I am not a perfect, fully self-evolved person, like those souls who have survived horrific trauma and say they've never wondered "why me?" I cannot claim that I never questioned God or the universe. There were times when I asked myself "why?" Not so much for my loss of my relationship with my mother or in a self-pitying way, but for the loss of my children's relationships with their grandmother and her relationship with them. Over the years, I'd come to realize that there is *no* answer and all I can do is to help them understand that my mother's choices—both with me and with them—are all that she's capable of making. It doesn't mean that she loves me or them any less than any other parent or grandparent, but it does mean that she cannot think beyond herself. And if you want to label that as selfish, narcissistic, or broken, that's on you.

And it is this reality that reminds me to always make the best decisions I can for my family to ensure that it is as strong and prepared to live and grab life as fully as possible so at the end, there are no regrets. Kent and I from the very start shared the same life motivations. We looked at life through the same lens, and as a result, connected on a very deep level. We both were extremely driven; he's worked tirelessly at the same multinational firm for more than 30 years to become one of the top financial advisors in the country, and counts celebrities and popular sports figures as some of his clients. And even though Kent did not have the same upbringing as I did (or the same challenges that I faced) his parents were definitely of an older generation with very different social attitudes than ours. His mother catered to his father and his father enjoyed every moment of it! He never complained and neither did Kent's mother, and that was the family dynamic Kent was accustomed to.

When he met me, a very strong-willed, strong-minded young woman, he wasn't sure how to react. I was opposite of his mother and would never kowtow to anyone who was able-bodied enough to care for themselves. I think that's also what attracted him to me. And I was attracted to him because he was strong, driven, smart, and a loyal, loving person. And although he is highly successful because of those traits, his work is not what defines him. He is a man of rare character, a man of a rare balance of traits that make him an achiever but also allow him to hold deep levels of compassion, sympathy, and objectivity.

§

After Kennedy's Frye boot and Free People jacket modeling incident, her closet raiding habit grew to a regular conversation on weekends.

Football season was always a major event in our house, and the boys would get lost in watching games on the family room TV as I did laundry for the whole family. Kennedy loved to sit on the bed with me, a giant pile of clothes warm from the dryer between us, and watch as I folded it.

"Mom! Can I borrow your shirt from South Moon Under? The one that's off-the-shoulder?" She looked at me with Precious Moments eyes so big and green that they took my breath away.

"Sure, honey," I said as I picked up the shirt and tossed it at her. South Moon Under was our favorite store and brought back memories of my youth when my mom and I would go clothes shopping.

"This shirt reminds me of the shirts my mom used to wear. She'd wear them with really tight acid-wash jeans and ankle boots. There was a really famous movie called *Flashdance* about a talented dancer trying to make it in the business, and her wardrobe in the movie created a fashion craze where women were cutting their sweatshirts into sleeveless, off-the-shoulder tops!"

I smiled a little smile as I remembered my mom modeling those pretty outfits around our apartment. Just like my own daughter was doing now. Kennedy grabbed the shirt and quickly threw it over her head, her smile growing bigger by the second. She let out a squeal and twirled around in front of the dressing mirror.

"Mom, can I ask you something?" Kennedy asked, suddenly quiet. The smile slowly disappeared from her perfect, innocent face.

"Sure, what's up?" I asked.

"Did you ever forgive Gigi?"

§

"Landslide" by Fleetwood Mac played on the Bose speaker and the melodies wafted over the deck.

The sun rose higher in the sky and a breeze picked up. It blew the wispy clouds in my view into nothingness until nothing but brilliant blue sky remained. I grabbed a fuzzy blanket to put over my legs. The cat moved from the shade where it once was warm to the direct sun by my feet to soak in its warmth and to be close to me.

I looked at the empty plate that until recently held some Asiago cheese and crackers.

"Hey Mom," I heard Kennedy say.

"Hiya Mom," Tye and Kolt said in unison as all three scrambled out onto the deck.

My silent time was broken by my children, as it was when they were infants and I begged for a few moments to sleep undisturbed. But now I welcomed the interruption.

The kids sat on the deck and Kolt slyly checked to see if I'd eaten my snack. He wanted my leftovers, but there weren't any. When he caught me as I caught him, he coughed suddenly.

"Mom, I think my screen is cracked. Can we go to the Apple store?" Kolt creaked. I think he felt a little self-conscious that he was recently eating everything in the house to fuel his growth spurt and bottomless boy stomach. He'd probably eat a stick of butter if that was all he could find!

"Sure honey, just put it on the calendar," I replied, knowing that Kolt would not let me forget.

Tye picked up the cat and cradled it in his arms.

"You're going to miss doing my laundry when I go to college, right Mom?" he joked.

I felt tears rising to the surface and turned away to hide them.

You have no idea, Tye. No idea.

I took a sip of wine and closed my eyes to drive the feelings down. I heard birds twittering near the tree house in the backyard and the chatter of my children. Kennedy leaned back against the soft cushion next to me on the patio couch and the boys sat across from us engrossed in their cell phones.

Yes, I have forgiven my mother, I thought. I don't know when it happened exactly, but it did. I broke the cycle, and yet it continued. Only now, the cycle was bigger and better than before. My mother would always be a part of my life, but as a phantom. I could only look forward now, toward my children and my life. I made it. We made it. *In spite of you and because of you.*

Thank you, Mom, wherever you are. I hope someday you find peace and learn how to love yourself.

BRIDGETTE PEARCE

ABOUT THE AUTHOR

BRIDGETTE PEARCE graduated from the University of Maryland, College Park, and helps others find the strength to move forward, one step at a time, from a place of love, not fear, hatred or resentment. As the owner of Empower You, LLC, she has a solid and enthusiastic website, Instagram and Facebook following that showcases her tour dates and motivational blog. She lives with her three children in Maryland.

www.iambridgette.com
IG b_empowered_
FB @empower.you.today

Made in the USA
Middletown, DE
28 February 2022